SECOND EDITION

the Marginal Teacher

A Step-by-Step Guide
to Fair Procedures for Identification
and Dismissal

C. Edward Lawrence

Myra K. Vachon

Donald O. Leake

Brenda H. Leake

CORWIN PRESS, INC.
A Sage Publications Company
Thousand Oaks, California

For information:

Corwin Press, Inc.
A Sage Publications Company
2455 Teller Road
Thousand Oaks, California 91320
E-mail: order@corwinpress.com

Sage Publications Ltd.
6 Bonhill Street
London EC2A 4PU
United Kingdom

Sage Publications India Pvt. Ltd.
M-32 Market
Greater Kailash I
New Delhi 110 048 India

Printed in the United States of America

Library of Congress Cataloging-in-Publication Data

The marginal teacher: A step-by-step guide to fair procedures for identification and dismissal / by C. Edward Lawrence ... [et al.].—2nd ed.
    p. cm.
Includes bibliographical references.
ISBN 0-7619-7767-8 (c: alk. paper) — ISBN 0-7619-7768-6 (p: alk. paper)
    1. Teachers—Rating of—United States. 2. Teachers—Dismissal of—United States. I. Lawrence, C. Edward.
LB2838 .M376 2000
371.14'4—dc21   00-011038

This book is printed on acid-free paper.

01 02 03 04 05 06 07 7 6 5 4 3 2 1

Editorial Assistant:	Kylee Liegl
Acquiring Editor:	Robb Clouse
Production Editor:	Diane S. Foster
Editorial Assistant:	Victoria Cheng
Typesetter/Designer:	D&G Limited, LLC
Indexer:	Kathy Paparchontis
Cover Designer:	Michael Dobowe

Contents

List of Sample Documents

(Even though some documents may be used more than once, they are listed only under the heading of the first month during which they are used.)

A Cautionary Note

This guidebook is not a legal document. It is intended to provide accurate information about the subject matter. It is sold with the understanding that the publisher and the authors are not engaged in rendering legal or other professional services. Specifically, the recommendations contained herein are guidelines only and not legal advice, and the publisher and the authors do not warrant, in any manner, their suitability for any particular usage. If legal advice or other expert assistance is required, the services of an attorney or other competent professional, with knowledge of all laws pertaining to the reader and the jurisdiction, should be sought.

Preface

Principals are often faced with the difficult decision whether to retain or dismiss a marginal classroom teacher. Because of the need to prepare sufficient documentation and for the presentation of the documentation at the various hearings, the teacher dismissal process is a time-consuming and emotionally draining experience for principals. When documentation has been inadequately prepared by principals, their recommendations for dismissal are usually overturned by the school board, an independent hearing officer, or the court system. The rejection of the recommendation for dismissal further intimidates the principals and their peers who then become even more apprehensive about pursuing the dismissal process in the future. As a result, the marginal teacher remains in the classroom, further damaging children who deserve the best education possible.

For the protection of our children, principals must have the knowledge and expertise to prepare for the documentation necessary for dismissing a marginal teacher. As educators who have worked with principals on a daily basis and served as hearing officers for teacher dismissal conferences, we recognized the need for a practical reference guide to assist principals in the process of teacher dismissal.

The Marginal Teacher: A Step-by-Step Guide to Fair Procedures for Identification and Dismissal correlates with two other books that we have written providing step-by-step procedures for handling tough personnel issues, such as staff misconduct, and evaluating school specialists (e.g., counselors, psychologists, librarians, and special education teachers). It is designed to be a comprehensive, practical approach to the teacher dismissal process and includes guidelines and procedures that will streamline the time-consuming and potentially frustrating task. The guidelines are accompanied by numerous tips to help principals avoid the pitfalls they might encounter as they proceed with the steps to dismiss the marginal teacher. In addition, the guide includes examples of letters, observation forms, checklists, a calendar with action dates identified, and a sample document that can be modified to fit individual school districts and situations.

Whereas the first edition of *The Marginal Teacher* included some writing of Dr. Donald O. Leake and Dr. Brenda H. Leake, this new edition reflects the writing of

Dr. C. Edward Lawrence and Dr. Myra K. Vachon, the first and second authors. This edition is based on feedback received from school districts and school administrators who commented that both the book and the electronic documents are essential tools for the busy principal; it has been simplified by focusing on the practical application of the teacher dismissal process. The authors have also incorporated additional examples of support and have clarified language in documents. In addition, all of the sample forms, checklists, calendars, and letters, as well as the sample teacher dismissal documentation, are provided on a CD-ROM and can be easily modified to fit individual situations.

The procedures are organized in a month-by-month and step-by-step format. We believe that the three-part process in *The Marginal Teacher* makes it easier for principals to dismiss the marginal teacher. In this process, principals must, first of all, establish and implement a consistent, schoolwide teacher evaluation process for all teachers, following contractual procedures, board policies, and state and federal laws. Second, principals must establish consistent procedures to identify the marginal teacher and develop a specific plan to provide intensive assistance to the marginal teacher. Last, principals must collect and prepare the documentation necessary to substantiate the recommendation for dismissal of the marginal teacher.

In the following list are examples of broad topics for the teacher dismissal process during each month:

August—Establishing the foundation by reviewing district policies and procedures related to evaluations, welcoming all staff back to school, and providing orientation sessions for new teachers

September—Informing all staff about the evaluation process and forms, conducting brief observations of all teachers to establish baseline data, and organizing necessary files

October—Issuing memoranda of concerns, conducting formal observations, holding feedback conferences, and initiating a plan of intensive assistance for marginal teachers

November—Continuing observations, documentation, and revisions of the assistance plan

December—Continuing observations, documentation, and implementing the assistance plan, contacting the district's attorney, and issuing the letter placing the teacher on notice of a potential unsatisfactory teacher evaluation

January—Organizing the documentation, obtaining historical information, writing the unsatisfactory evaluation, preparing for the unsatisfactory evaluation conference, and conducting the unsatisfactory evaluation conference

February through June—Preparing for conferences beyond the school level, completing the evaluation process for all teachers, and preparing for the next school year

We are not implying that the examples used in *The Marginal Teacher* are the only methods or procedures or that the process is the only or even the best process to follow. This model is intended to illustrate how the actions of principals can be integrated with the evaluation system in a consistent and coherent manner. The sample forms that are provided should be adapted and modified to fit the needs and guidelines of individual school districts. Therefore, it is essential that principals thoroughly review their own district's evaluation procedures, including stipulations in the teachers' contract, before using this or any other guide.

We sincerely appreciate the many administrators and clinical supervision students who shared their experiences. Their ideas laid the foundation for the development of the process and forms provided in *The Marginal Teacher*. The variety of forms and letters are a compendium of our collective experiences in instructional supervision. Although we were unable to acknowledge each individual contribution, any similarity in existing material is purely unintended. In addition, we extend a special thanks to colleagues who reacted to the contents of the guide and used these step-by-step procedures as a model for the documentation they prepared to successfully dismiss marginal teachers. Their efforts will ensure that only the competent teachers remain in the classroom to teach our most precious resources—our children. Last, we acknowledge the support, encouragement, and editorial assistance provided by the staff at Corwin Press, especially Gracia Alkema during the first edition and Robert Clouse during the second edition.

About the Authors

C. Edward Lawrence is a Clinical Professor in the Department of Instructional and Curricular Studies at the University of Nevada, Las Vegas. He earned a bachelor's degree in Elementary Education from West Virginia State College, a master's degree in Guidance and Counseling from Marquette University, and a Certificate in Administrative Leadership and a PhD in Urban Education from the University of Wisconsin-Milwaukee. Prior to his present position, he was Assistant Superintendent, where he had an extensive career in education. He served as a teacher; counselor; team leader; assistant principal on the elementary, middle, and high school levels; elementary and middle school principal; director of alternative programs; and community superintendent. He also has been a hearing officer for the evaluation of unsatisfactory teachers, second-step misconduct cases, and immediate staff suspensions. In addition, he has consulted with school districts on how to prepare and sustain unsatisfactory teacher evaluation and misconduct cases. He is coauthor (with Myra K. Vachon) of *The Marginal Teacher: A Step-by-Step Guide to Fair Procedures for Identification and Dismissal* (1993). His other publications (with Myra K. Vachon) are *How to Handle Staff Misconduct: A Step-by-Step Guide* (1995) and *The Incompetent Specialist: How to Evaluate, Document Performance, and Dismiss School Staff* (1996).

Myra K. Vachon is an educational consultant who recently retired from the position of Executive Director of Human Resources for a large urban school district. She earned a bachelor's degree in Secondary Education, a master's degree in Curriculum and Instruction, a Certificate in Administrative Leadership, and a PhD in Urban Education from the University of Wisconsin-Milwaukee. She also earned certification as Professional in Human Resources from the Society of Human Resources Management. She has served as a teacher, department chairman, curriculum and instruction supervisor, school administrator, and assistant to community superintendent, Leadership Specialist, Director of Staffing Services, and Executive Director of Human Resources. She has supervised preservice and inservice classroom teachers, served as a hearing officer for second- and third-step misconducts, advised principals regarding teacher supervision procedures and techniques, and conducted workshops for school administrators on how to prepare and sustain unsatisfactory teacher evaluations and misconduct cases. She has also served as adjunct instructor at Alverno College-Milwaukee in the Education Department, teaching an elementary science methods course, and at the University of Wisconsin-Milwaukee in the Department of Administrative Leadership, teaching a course in clinical supervision. She is coauthor (with C. Edward Lawrence) of *The Marginal Teacher: A Step-by-Step Guide to Fair Procedures for Identification and Dismissal* (1993). Her other publications (with C. Edward Lawrence) are *How to Handle Staff Misconduct: A Step-by-Step Guide* (1995) and *The Incompetent Specialist: How to Evaluate, Document Performance, and Dismiss School Staff* (1996). Other publications include "The Other C&I," "Analysis of an Eighth Grade Science Textbook," and *A Method for Determining the Level of Abstraction of Science Reading Material.*

Introduction

As a principal, how do you inform a teacher that his or her performance is unacceptable? How do you make a decision to recommend termination? This step-by-step dismissal process is predicated on the following four assumptions:

1. You have established administrative and instructional credibility with the staff.
2. You have effectively monitored the instructional climate in all classrooms, and you have provided assistance to those teachers who are having difficulties.
3. You know the physical and psychological demands inherent in the dismissal process. (The additional time and energy required to document a marginal teacher's deficiencies are immense; therefore, you must be committed to following through with the process.)
4. You have discussed the process with individuals in central administration as well as the attorney for the school district to obtain their support and to ensure that legal and contractual obligations are met.

By following the procedures outlined in the month-by-month steps, you can proceed with the assurance that you have met the due process requirements, have provided ample opportunity for the teacher to improve to a satisfactory level, and have the necessary documentation to substantiate a recommendation for dismissal. The following chapters are designed to help you work through the process to dismiss the marginal teacher who has been provided with intensive assistance but who has failed to improve his or her teaching performance. Each of the following chapters provides suggested protocol, sample forms, sample letters, and administrative tips to facilitate the process.

Throughout the nation, the dismissal rate of teachers for unsatisfactory teaching performance is very low because many principals fear the dismissal process. Some principals believe that when a teacher is granted tenure, he or she cannot be dismissed unless the teacher is involved in serious misconduct. On the contrary, nontenured and tenured teachers can be dismissed for ineffective teaching performance. The principal must conduct a sufficient number of classroom observations, intervene to assess the teacher's performance, make suggestions for improvements, provide remedial assistance to the teacher, and give a specific date for the teacher to demonstrate improvement to a satisfactory level. Consistent with the preestablished time line, the principal must assess the teacher's ability to meet the suggestions to improve his or her teaching performance. If the teacher has not shown improvement, then the principal recommends to the superintendent of schools that the teacher be terminated. It is the superintendent of schools who notifies the school board to schedule a board meeting to hear the termination case. In addition, the superintendent sends a letter to the teacher stating his or her decision to recommend the teacher's termination to the school board. After the board hears the case, and if the board confirms the superintendent's recommendation, then a letter is sent to the teacher informing him or her that the board has agreed with the superintendent's recommendation to terminate his or her services from the XYZ school district. Moreover, the superintendent of schools is not required to give reasons for terminating the nontenured teacher's services.

Although dismissing a teacher is time consuming, principals use this as an excuse to point fingers to blame the teachers' union for protecting ineffective teachers. The job of the teachers' union representative is to defend the teacher and protect the teacher's job. The union does not protect the rights of children to receive a good education. It is the role of the principal to ensure that children have only the best teachers in their classrooms.

To reduce the principal's fears about the dreaded teacher evaluation process, school districts must develop procedures and time lines, incorporating just-cause requirements and due process. As a result, teachers will be unable to initiate legal action based on race, gender, or age discrimination. In addition, teachers will be unable to make accusations that principals retaliated against them for filing lawsuits. Principals must see that employee rights are not violated so that that a third-party hearing officer, an arbitrator, or the civil court does not overturn a teacher dismissal. Accordingly, principals must be able to answer "yes" to the following 10 questions, to ensure that the teacher's just-cause requirements have been met:

1. Was the evaluation process for the school district made known to all teachers working at the school(s)?
2. Was the evaluation process consistently applied to all teachers?
3. Was the teacher treated consistently with other teachers and not singled out?
4. Did the observations include all phases of the teacher's assignment, morning and afternoon?
5. Was there a continuous and accurately dated file of all conferences with and observations of the teacher?
6. Did the teacher receive written memoranda of concerns specifying exact deficiencies?

7. In each memorandum of concerns given to the teacher, did the teacher receive a list of specific suggestions for correcting deficiencies and ways to achieve a satisfactory level of performance?

8. Was an intensive assistance plan established and implemented for the teacher, using school and district resources?

9. Was the teacher given a reasonable period of time to improve teaching performance?

10. Was the teacher informed in writing that failure to achieve an acceptable level of performance by a specified date would result in the issuance of an unsatisfactory evaluation?

If you can answer "yes" to these questions, you have a greater chance of winning a teacher dismissal.

Because of the amount of time, energy, and documentation that is required to dismiss an ineffective teacher, the steps provided in this guidebook are essential activities to meet just-cause requirements and to ensure that due process was followed. And a reminder: In dealing with marginal teachers, feelings on all sides can run high, and an indiscreet comment can create chaos. Avoid social relationships with teachers or any staff members, and choose your confidantes outside the school milieu. Furthermore, you must never become romantically involved with a teacher or another staff member. Not only would such rumors be likely to surface during the evaluation process, but during any dismissal hearings, they might explode in the media.

1
Describing the Marginal Teacher

The marginal teacher lacks the skill to ensure an efficient, orderly classroom and a safe learning environment for students.

When asked to describe a "good" teacher, students consistently identify knowledge, skills, abilities, and attitudes. Those characteristics most commonly listed by students in classrooms in which we have taught include the following:

- Is patient
- Is enthusiastic
- Is well organized
- Is clear
- Likes students
- Is resourceful
- Knows the subject
- Is empathetic
- Is fair
- Fosters creativity
- Is dedicated
- Is sensitive

- Is flexible
- Is task orientated
- Fosters cooperation
- Respects students
- Is consistent in treatment of students
- Has good motivational, communications, and classroom management skills
- Uses good human relations techniques
- Uses a variety of questioning techniques
- Is available to students and parents
- Believes that he or she can make a difference

Principals have stated that they expect all teachers to conduct themselves as professionals to ensure the efficient, orderly operation of the school and to provide a safe learning environment for students. Basically, this means that they report to work on time, perform their assigned duties, attend staff meetings, and follow reasonable administrative directives.

Although classroom observation is essential in evaluating the performance of teachers, you can easily recognize where problem areas are even without going into the classroom. For example, you can use indicators such as the following:

- Number of student discipline referrals
- Number of complaints from students, parents, or other staff members
- Number of students receiving failing grades
- Attitude (e.g., resistance to change, uncooperativeness with other staff members, refusal to do what is expected)

A marginal teacher is borderline between competent and incompetent. The marginal teacher may do enough just to get by for an evaluation but then slip back into a chronic pattern of poor teaching. This ineffective teaching may be the result of inadequate training, personal problems that interfere with effective teaching performance, simply a negative attitude, or some combination of these. Poor performance consists of a lack of preparation, deficiencies in teaching skills, problems with classroom management, poor judgment, and absences from school. The marginal teacher seems unable or unwilling to improve his or her teaching performance and thus has a negative impact on students.

The marginal teacher may demonstrate any combination of the following characteristics:

- Consumes too much administrative time
- Displays a negative attitude toward teaching

- Does not adequately supervise students
- Does not follow school procedures and guidelines
- Does not follow the adopted curriculum
- Does not get students actively involved in classroom presentations
- Does not maintain appropriate scope and sequence
- Does not maintain classroom decorum
- Does not prepare adequately
- Does not provide a safe learning environment
- Does not use instructional time efficiently
- Does not communicate effectively with parents
- Engages in power struggles with students
- Has a disproportionate number of student discipline referrals
- Has a limited range of instructional strategies
- Has inadequate or no lesson plans
- Has an excessive number of students receiving failing marks
- Has numerous complaints from students, parents, and colleagues in the building
- Has poor classroom management skills
- Inadequately reinforces learning
- Is resistant to change
- Is uncooperative with other staff members
- Lacks communication skills
- Lacks organizational skills
- Presents boring lessons
- Uses an excessive number of worksheets
- Uses an irrational grading system
- Has a negative attitude and refuses to do what is expected

By following the steps in this guide, you will be able to provide assistance to the teacher and hopefully bring about a positive change in performance or, if necessary, use the documentation to substantiate a recommendation for termination because of poor teaching performance.

Establishing the Teacher Evaluation Process

The most difficult problem in school administration today is dealing with the employment and dismissal of incompetent teachers. It's easier to appoint a marginal teacher than to dismiss one.

—Unknown, 1906

Suggested Timeline: August

Step 1 in the evaluation process of the marginal teacher involves the same sound procedures that you should follow for your entire staff. Before the new school year begins, a plan must be developed for welcoming staff members and providing orientation to the school. This step sets a positive tone for staff members by informing the new teachers and reminding teachers returning to the school about overall expectations, responsibilities, and procedures. Frequently, the small things make the difference between a successful and an unsuccessful school year. You must take the leadership role in providing the necessary support to ensure a successful school opening.

During August, the following procedures should occur:

❑ Send a welcome letter to all staff assigned to the building (see Sample Document 2.1).

❑ Assign a mentor teacher to each new teacher, and identify the mentor teacher in a welcome letter to the new teacher (see Sample Document 2.2).

❏ Provide orientation for mentor teachers assigned to assist new teachers that includes the following:

1. A review of specific building rules and procedures
2. A suggested timeline for the mentor teacher to interact with the new teacher
3. A discussion of "what ifs" (e.g., what if the new teacher is experiencing problems with classroom management or what if the new teacher and mentor teacher are incompatible)
4. Suggestions regarding the type of assistance the mentor teacher can provide the new teacher
5. A copy of the teacher handbook, for the mentor teacher to help the new teacher

❏ Provide an orientation session for all new teachers that includes

1. A tour of the building
2. An overview of instructional resources available within the school
3. An introduction to support staff members
4. Suggestions for strategies to meet and communicate with parents or guardians

❏ Conduct an orientation session for the entire staff (e.g., teaching assistants, secretary, engineer) highlighting the educational philosophy of the school, the district goals, expectations for staff and volunteers, and general procedures, including classroom management, lesson plans, maintenance of records, and duty schedules. Also,

1. Display a welcome-back banner (e.g., This will be the best school year!).
2. Have all teachers introduce themselves, tell what they teach, and give a brief statement about what they did during the summer.
3. Encourage staff to have bulletin boards in place no later than the first week of school.
4. Cater a lunch or set up a potluck lunch for staff. (Include information about this activity in the welcome-back letter, and have staff call the school secretary regarding the dishes they plan to bring.)

❏ To ensure that due process relative to teacher dismissal is followed and the property rights of the teacher are not violated, review contractual language, school board policies, state statutes, and the U.S. Constitution (e.g., the 14th Amendment).

❏ Develop an orientation plan for students new to the building at the beginning of the school year as well as students who transfer into the building during the year.

Sample Document 2.1
Letter Welcoming Staff
(Place on school letterhead)

Date

Dear Staff:

I hope you are having a restful and pleasant summer vacation. The 20__ school year will present new challenges to all of us—new students, new teachers, and new textbooks and instructional materials.

This school year, we will rededicate our efforts to provide an excellent education for all of our students. As always, we will continue to work together to make our school the best in the _____ School District.

In preparation for our first meeting of the school year, I am enclosing a copy of the organization day agenda. I am very enthusiastic about working with you this school year to meet the greater challenges ahead in educating our children—our most precious resources.

Again, welcome back! This will be the best year ever at _____ School.

Sincerely,

_____

Principal

Enclosures

Sample Document 2.2
Letter Assigning a Mentor Teacher to Each
New and Transfer Teacher
(Place on school letterhead)

Date

Name of Teacher
Address

Dear _____:

Welcome to _____ School. I want to make this an educationally rewarding and successful school year for you. This will be the best year ever for staff and students at _____ School.

To help you adjust to your new school, I have assigned _____ in room ___ to serve as your mentor teacher, to answer questions you may have about the school and to assist you throughout the school year. I am also here to assist you in any way possible to make this a successful school year. Please feel free to contact me to discuss any concerns you may have.

Again, welcome to _____ School. I am happy to have you join our staff, and I look forward to observing the exciting learning activities in your classroom.

Sincerely,

_____
Principal

cc: Mentor Teacher

3 *Beginning the Evaluation Process*

Too many principals are reluctant to handle tough personnel issues because of fables told about other principals who fired teachers only to have the school board rehire the teachers, pay them months of back wages, and change the evaluation, forcing the principal to issue an apology letter promising not to retaliate against the teachers.

Suggested Time Line: September

If you adhere to a teacher evaluation process as defined in state statutes, contractual obligations, and school district policies, you should have no fear of the teacher dismissal process. But because of this fear, some principals prolong the problems by changing the teacher's assignment by giving him or her a smaller class. Or the principal may add a teaching assistant to help the teacher. Other principals eliminate an educational program to transfer the teacher out of the school. Still other principals examine the teacher's certification and add an area in which the teacher is not certified to teach; therefore, the teacher must be transferred to another school. Yet other principals put up with the ineffective teacher for the entire school year, holding a bitter year-end conference with the teacher about his or her poor teaching. Sometimes, the principal candidly tells the teacher that he or she will receive an unsatisfactory evaluation if he or she returns to school next year.

As a result of the foregoing actions by the principals, marginal teachers are transferred from school to school, and the poor teaching continues. Then, principals feel that they have successfully performed their job of getting rid of those ineffective teachers. In turn, principals blame the teachers' union and the school district personnel office for transferring the ineffective teacher into their school the following year. But principals must remember that just as they forced an ineffective teacher out of their schools, other principals are doing the same. Thus the "dance of the lemons" continues year after year as the ineffective teacher moves from one school to another. Instead, principals must collectively learn the step-by-step procedures to remove or terminate marginal teachers from their school districts. During Step 2, the principal must do the following five things:

1. Inform all teachers about the evaluation process.
2. Identify the teachers' official evaluator.
3. Initiate a system for providing ongoing instructional support to all staff.
4. Conduct brief observations in all classrooms.
5. Set up a filing system to accumulate various forms of documentation that reflect the performance of each teacher.

During September, the following procedures should occur:

❏ Provide to the teaching staff a written explanation of the evaluation process, with sample formal and informal evaluation instruments that will be used to evaluate them (see Sample Documents 3.1, 3.2, and 3.3).

❏ Prepare individualized letters to teachers identifying you, the principal, as the evaluator and a roster for teachers to initial showing receipt of the letter (see Documents 3.4 and 3.5).

❏ *Hand deliver* the evaluator identification letter to each teacher and have teachers initial receipt of their letters (see Sample Documents 3.4 and 3.5). Because you may need proof that a teacher received his or evaluation letter, do not place it in the teachers' mailboxes.

❏ Begin conducting daily observations to identify teachers who may be experiencing classroom problems, and maintain a summary form of informal classroom observations (see Sample Document 3.6).

❏ Plan to provide written feedback to the teacher within five school days of making an informal classroom observation.

❏ During classroom visits, collect samples of assignments that teachers give to students to ensure that the work meets district standards, and keep these samples in individual teacher files.

❏ If the quality of work samples is poor or if classroom management is poor, write a memorandum of concerns to the teacher and offer suggestions for improvement.

❏ Prepare a parental complaint file (both verbal and written) for each teacher (see Sample Documents 3.7 and 3.8).

❏ Keep copies of all notes written to you by the teacher about his or her discipline problems or other school-related issues.

❑ Maintain a record of the number of pending suspensions, suspensions, letters sent to parents, and other disciplinary actions requested by the teacher.

❑ Record the number of students referred to the office for disrupting the class, including the date, time, reason, the teacher's comments and recommendation, as well as the administrative disposition (see Sample Document 3.9).

❑ Provide teaching tips in the weekly staff bulletin.

❑ Hold grade-level meetings for all teachers.

❑ Work in collaboration with the assistant principal or central administration staff who can conduct teacher evaluations; however, remember that you should be the sole evaluator.

❑ Record each parental complaint on a standard parental complaint form and discuss the complaint with the teacher. Following your deliberation, forward a copy of the parental complaint form with your disposition to the teacher for his or her response. File both copies (see Sample Documents 3.7 and 3.8).

❑ For serious parent complaints, use the misconduct provision of the contract, if one exists, for handling these situations (see Lawrence & Vachon, 1995, pp. 26-28).

❑ Be aware of the quantity of busywork (e.g., photocopies) given to students.

❑ Take photographs in the classroom or videotape lessons, particularly if the teacher is experiencing classroom management problems.

❑ Base your evaluation on firsthand observations of the teacher, not on hearsay.

❑ Complete all sections of the observation or evaluation form that apply to the specific observation and proofread the document for spelling and grammatical errors before signing it (see Sample Documents 3.2 and 3.3).

Sample Document 3.1
Letter Explaining the Evaluation Process
(Place on school letterhead)

Date

Dear Staff:

This year, three different approaches will be used to evaluate teachers. The informal, formal, and year-end teacher observation/evaluations will be used. Descriptions of these procedures follow.

Informal Observations/Evaluations (Formative)

Informal observations/evaluations will consist of short classroom observations and evaluations. An observation checklist will be used to give teachers immediate feedback on their performance. Teachers should expect more than three informal observations.

Formal Observations/Evaluations (Formative)

Formal observations/evaluations will be conducted for teachers scheduled for the district-mandated evaluation. A formal evaluation may be used for unscheduled teacher evaluations.

A formal evaluation will be scheduled for the duration of the class period; however, it may be shorter. Teachers scheduled for a formal evaluation are to schedule two preobservation conferences and two postobservation conferences.

During the preobservation conference, teachers are to explain their lesson plans and the methodology they plan to use in the lesson. The preobservation conference should take about 15 minutes. At the preobservation conference, teachers will receive a formal observation/evaluation form. Before the postobservation conference, teachers are to complete this form by checking the column that they believe best describes their teaching.

Within five days after the formal observation/evaluation, a postobservation conference should be held. During this conference, the teacher's strengths and weaknesses and suggestions for improvement, if necessary, will be discussed.

Year-End Evaluation (Summative)

This is the final observation/evaluation conference of the school year. This conference will be held during April or May. A written statement will be placed on the official district evaluation form.

Enclosed are copies of evaluation instruments that will be used to evaluate your teaching performance this year. If you have any questions, please see my secretary to schedule a meeting with me.

Sincerely,

_____

Principal

Enclosures

Sample Document 3.2
Informal Observation/Evaluation Form

_____ SCHOOL

INFORMAL OBSERVATION/EVALUATION FORM

Date _____ Time of day _____ Class period _____

Teacher _____ Subject/Grade _____

Total students assigned to class/In class ___ / ___ Evaluation number ___

Scale: 1 = *Outstanding*   3 = *Average*   5 = *Unsatisfactory*
        2 = *Above average* 4 = *Fair*   NA = *Not Applicable*

(NOTE: Insert criteria established by the school district.)

Criteria	1	2	3	4	5	NA
1.						
2.						
3.						
4.						
5.						
6.						
7.						
8.						
9.						
10.						
11.						
12.						

Comments _____

_____

If you wish to discuss this observation/evaluation checklist with me, please see my secretary to schedule an appointment with me.

Principal _____

Sample Document 3.3
Formal Observation/Evaluation Form
_____ SCHOOL
FORMAL OBSERVATION/EVALUATION FORM

Date _____ Time of day _____ Class period _____
Teacher _____ Subject/Grade _____
Total students assigned to class/In class ____ / ____ Evaluation number ____

Scale: 1 = *Outstanding*   3 = *Average*   5 = *Unsatisfactory*
         2 = *Above average*   4 = *Fair*   NA = *Not Applicable*

(NOTE: Insert specific criteria under the general categories, based on district standards.)

A. PLANNING/INSTRUCTIONAL STRATEGIES USED	1	2	3	4	5	NA
1.						
2.						
3.						
4.						
5.						

Comments _____
_____
_____

B. UNDERSTANDING THE CURRICULUM	1	2	3	4	5	NA
1.						
2.						
3.						
4.						
5.						

Comments _____
_____
_____

C. ASSESSMENT OF INSTRUCTIONAL PLAN	1	2	3	4	5	NA
1.						
2.						
3.						
4.						
5.						

Comments _____

_____

_____

D. CLASSROOM MANAGEMENT	1	2	3	4	5	NA
1.						
2.						
3.						
4.						
5.						

Comments _____

_____

_____

E. CLASSROOM ENVIRONMENT	1	2	3	4	5	NA
1.						
2.						
3.						
4.						
5.						

Comments _____

_____

_____

F. SCHOOLWIDE INVOLVEMENT	1	2	3	4	5	NA
List your involvement in school activities:						

1. _____

2. _____

3. _____

Comments _____

_____

_____

G. PROFESSIONAL DEVELOPMENT	1	2	3	4	5	NA
List your involvement in professional development activities:						

1. _____

2. _____

3. _____

Comments _____

_____

_____

If you wish to discuss this observation/evaluation checklist with me, please see my secretary to schedule an appointment with me.

Principal _____

Sample Document 3.4
Letter Identifying the Teacher's Evaluator
(Place on school letterhead)

Date

Name of Teacher
School Address

Dear _____ :

The primary purpose of performance evaluation is to improve teaching performance and promote professional growth. This is consistent with the contract between the _____ Board of School Directors and the (name of the bargaining unit). The evaluation procedures for this school year will ensure that a cooperative plan is established by the teacher and the evaluator.

Teacher evaluations are a necessary part of educational administration. They should be viewed by teachers as a learning experience, as a way for both the teacher and the administrator to grow in understanding and knowledge

Teacher strengths will be discussed so that they can enhance the learning environment and to further professional development. Teacher weaknesses will be identified so that appropriate methods can be devised to reduce or alleviate those weaknesses.

Part _____, Section _____ of the _____ contract states that the identification of the evaluator must be made known to the teacher by name and title. Accordingly, you are informed that your performance evaluation during the 20XX-20XX school year shall be conducted by me, with possible collaboration with other administrative and supervisory staff assigned to _____ School. In the event that someone else must serve in my capacity, that person will conduct your evaluation.

Sincerely,

_____
Principal

Sample Document 3.5
Roster for Teacher Initials Acknowledging
Receipt of Letter Identifying the Evaluator
(Place on school letterhead)

_____ SCHOOL
STAFF ROSTER
20 ___ - ___

INITIAL   NAME _____

_____   _____

_____   _____

_____   _____

_____   _____

_____   _____

_____   _____

_____   _____

_____   _____

_____   _____

_____   _____

_____   _____

_____   _____

_____   _____

_____   _____

_____   _____

_____   _____

_____   _____

_____   _____

_____   _____

_____   _____

_____   _____

_____   _____

_____   _____

_____   _____

Sample Document 3.6
Summary Form for Formal and Informal Classroom Observations

As the principal, you must begin the evaluation process by conducting informal observations of all classrooms throughout the school day. To assess the effectiveness of all teachers and the quality of teaching, you should use a monitoring form to document the number of informal observations conducted during the month of September. The same form should be adjusted and used for each month. Formal observations should also be documented on this form.

Procedures

❏ Use a monthly summary form to record the dates that informal classroom observations are conducted of all teachers.

❏ Identify teachers who may be in need of instructional support.

SUMMARY OF FORMAL AND INFORMAL CLASSROOM OBSERVATIONS
_____, 20 ___

SCHOOL _____   PRINCIPAL _____

Insert the dates that school is in session along the top row and the names of all teaching staff members in the first column. Place a check mark in the grid to indicate that an observation was made. Circle the check mark for a formal observation.

STAFF MEMBER																								

Sample Document 3.7
Parental Complaint Form

You must have a procedure for recording and maintaining a parental complaint file that can be used to support an unsatisfactory teacher evaluation. Moreover, you must know and follow the contractual procedures for handling parental complaints in your school district. This includes informing the teacher of the nature of the parental complaint, investigating the complaint, resolving the complaint, giving a copy of the disposition to the teacher, and maintaining copies of all related documents in a parental complaint file. For serious parental complaints, use the misconduct provision of the contract, if one exists. You will also need to determine if the teacher's actions warrant immediate suspension from teaching duties (Lawrence & Vachon, 1995, pp. 12–13) and follow appropriate steps.

Procedures

❑ Use a standard parental complaint form to register a parental complaint.

❑ Follow contractual procedures for informing the teacher and obtaining additional information regarding the complaint.

❑ Resolve the complaint.

❑ For serious parental complaints, use the misconduct provision of the contract, if one exists.

❑ Keep a copy of the parental complaint with your disposition as well as a copy of the teacher's response.

❑ Maintain a parental complaint file.

_____ SCHOOL PARENTAL COMPLAINT FORM

Date _____   Time _____ A.M./P.M.

Student _____   Grade _____ ID Number _____

Address _____

Person Filing Complaint _____

Relationship to Student _____

Phone Number: Home _____   Other _____

Nature of Complaint _____
_____
_____
_____

Action Requested _____
_____

Has a Previous Complaint Been Filed? Yes _____ No _____ Date(s) _____

Person(s) Spoken with:

_____
Name/Title/Department

_____
Name/Title/Department

Resolution _____
_____
_____
_____
_____

Complaint Resolved _____ Further Action Necessary _____

_____   _____
Signature/Title   Date

Sample Document 3.8
Parental Complaint Letter
(Place on school letterhead)

Date

Name of Teacher
School Address

Dear _____ :

Part ____, Section ____ of the _____ School District Contract states
that when parental or public complaints are filed, the individual teacher must be
made aware of the complaint. Therefore I am forwarding the enclosed
letter/parental complaint form received about you on _____, 20 ____.

Please plan to meet in my office on _____, 20 ____, at ____ P.M., to discuss
this parental complaint. If this time is inconvenient, please contact my secretary
to reschedule the meeting. We must resolve this complaint by _____, 20 ____.

Sincerely,

_____
Principal

Enclosure

Sample Document 3.9
Summary of Student Discipline Referrals

The following disciplinary referrals from _____ were sent to the principal, assistant principal, or dean to resolve:

Date	Time	Teacher Comments	Teacher Recommendations	Administrative Disposition

4 Identifying Teachers in Need of Assistance

Identify the marginal teacher early in the school year to allow time to provide support and assistance and to give teachers a reasonable length of time to improve their teaching performance.

Suggested Time Line: October

After a series of brief observations, you will identify the teachers who are having problems. Step 3 focuses on strategies to provide intensive assistance to those teachers who are experiencing difficulties. It is important to note that all teachers should remain in the overall supervision/evaluation process. However, additional support should be provided to the marginal teacher, and accurate and complete documentation must be maintained. You must assume the leadership role in assisting teachers needing support. Providing intensive assistance to marginal teachers is essential because

- It gives the teacher an opportunity to improve.

- It demonstrates your willingness to help the teacher.

- It is a necessary part of just cause.

At the beginning of the school year, you should conduct daily classroom observations of all teachers to identify teachers having teaching difficulties. You can easily recognize the marginal teacher who is having difficulties with classroom management. The classroom is disorderly and the teacher is unable to teach. You must provide this teacher with classroom teaching and management strategies.

You must conduct observations (both formal and informal) and conduct postobservation conferences to discuss your concerns about the teacher's classroom. After the meeting, you can send the teacher a letter summarizing the meeting and the discussion of the teacher's deficiencies. We recommend that you take a formal approach by sending a memorandum of concerns that lists teaching deficiencies and provides suggestions for improving teaching methods. This memorandum of concerns serves as the documentation that shows you notified the teacher about his or her teaching deficiencies and that you suggested ways for the teacher to improve his or her teaching methods.

The memorandum of concerns must be clear, free of spelling and grammatical errors, and should not contain educational jargon. Your language must be appropriate for third-party readers (e.g., an impartial hearing officer, a school board member, a judge) who must make decisions on written documentation. Equally important, you do not want the teacher's representative to point out your poor grammar or spelling errors or release your memorandum to school board members and the media. See Resource A for examples of descriptors that may be used to describe teaching performance problems.

By providing support and assistance to the teacher, you are meeting three just-cause requirements for a sustainable unsatisfactory teacher evaluation case.

During October, the following procedures should occur:

❏ Continue conducting daily observations in all classrooms to identify teachers who may be experiencing classroom problems.

❏ Prior to formal observations of teachers receiving intensive assistance, hold a preobservation conference with each teacher to discuss his or her lesson plans and the expected outcomes for the lesson you will observe.

❏ Conduct four formal observations, provide feedback listing areas of weakness and suggestions for improvement, and give a reasonable length of time for necessary improvements. If there is an assistant principal, he or she should also make daily visits and conduct informal observations. Determine if the teacher satisfied your suggestions for improvement (see Sample Documents 3.2 and 3.3).

❏ Following classroom observations, write a memorandum of concerns listing suggestions for improvements. Then hold a postobservation conference to discuss the concerns and to give a reasonable length of time for necessary improvements (see Sample Document 4.1).

❏ Provide an opportunity for the teacher to observe another teacher in the same school (see Sample Document 4.2 and 4.3).

❏ Provide an opportunity for the teacher to shadow a successful teacher at another school for an entire day (see Sample Document 4.4).

❏ Provide an opportunity for a teacher from another school to work for a day in the teacher's classroom (see Sample Document 4.5).

❏ Refer the teacher to sections in the teachers' handbook (e.g., classroom management; lesson planning; school procedures, such as referring students to the administration for disciplinary reasons) (see Sample Document 4.6).

❏ Refer the teacher to Web sites for information regarding teaching strategies, including cooperative learning, questioning, and classroom management (see Sample Document 4.7).

❏ Provide the teacher with sample lesson plans that outline key instructional behaviors for teaching a lesson.

❏ Provide a series of videotapes about effective teaching and classroom management (see Sample Document 4.8).

❏ Request clarification from the teacher about his or her classroom procedures (see Sample Document 4.9).

❏ Provide the teacher with journal articles on classroom management (see Sample Document 4.10).

❏ Provide the teacher with information about ordering professional books and references that will help improve teaching strategies and classroom management (see Sample Document 4.11).

❏ Refer the teacher to the weekly bulletin (see Sample Document 4.12).

❏ Provide opportunities for the teacher to attend workshops conducted by the school district (see Sample Document 4.13).

❏ Examine the teacher convention booklet to identify workshops to recommend that the teacher to attend (see Sample Document 4.14).

❏ Check to see if the teacher enrolled in the suggested workshops/classes.

❏ If the teacher does not improve, issue a letter summarizing the post-observation conference (see Sample Document 4.15).

❏ If the teacher shows improvement, note this on the observation form but re-emphasize the suggestions for improvement that you previously gave to the teacher.

❏ Take your incoming school mail into the classroom to scan while conducting informal classroom observations. Resist the temptation of letting these minor tasks interfere with the major task of documenting the teacher's performance.

❏ Take pictures in the classroom or videotape lessons, particularly if the teacher is experiencing classroom management problems.

❏ During staff meetings, encourage teachers to share successful teaching techniques and information on classroom management.

❏ Continue using the weekly staff bulletin to provide tips on teaching techniques and strategies for classroom management. This will help document your attempt to give assistance to the teaching staff.

❏ Continue maintaining a parental complaint file (for both verbal and written complaints) for each teacher (see Sample Documents 3.7 and 3.8).

❏ Continue examining samples of assignments that teachers give to students to make sure that they conform to district standards, and keep copies of these samples in individual teacher files.

❏ Continue monitoring the quantity of busywork (e.g., photocopies) that teachers give to students.

❏ Write another memorandum of concerns about poor classroom management, quality of work samples, and so forth (see Sample Document 4.1).

❏ Continue keeping copies of all notes that the teacher writes to you about his or her discipline problems or other school-related issues.

❏ Continue to maintain a record of the number of students referred to the office for disrupting the class, including the date, time, reason, teacher's comments, teacher's recommendation, and administrative disposition (see Sample Document 3.9).

❏ Write a letter to the teacher reviewing assistance provided to him or her (see Sample Document 4.16).

❏ Send a potential unsatisfactory evaluation update letter to your supervisor (see Sample Document 4.17).

❏ Prepare an unsatisfactory evaluation binder with a cover page, a table of contents, and a divider for each section (see Sample Documents 4.18 and 4.19).

❏ Check pertinent historical information about the teacher's background in the district (see Sample Document 4.20).

Sample Document 4.1
Memorandum of Concerns
(Place on school letterhead)

DATE:
TO:
FROM:
RE: Concerns and Suggestions for Improvement

This memorandum of concerns is about your teaching effectiveness, and it offers suggestions for improvement.

Concern 1:

Suggestions:

Concern 2:

Suggestions:

Concern 3:

Suggestions:

I stand ready to support you in improving your teaching performance, but improvement clearly rests with you. Please contact my secretary to schedule a meeting if you wish to discuss this memorandum of concerns with me.

Sample Document 4.2
Letter Confirming Arrangements
for the Teacher to Visit
a Classroom in the Same School
(Place on school letterhead)

Date

Name of Teacher and
School Address

Dear _____:

Because it is important for you to improve your teaching performance, especially classroom management, I would like you to visit _____'s classroom to observe

> (List specific activities, e.g., reading group, classroom management, instructional techniques.)

I have made arrangements for _____ to teach your class on ____ from ____ to ____.

During your observation, please use the enclosed Peer Observation Form as a guide to comment on the teacher's rules, procedures, and routines pertaining to classroom organization and management; instructional grouping strategies; and method for closing the lesson and transitioning to the next lesson.

We will discuss your observation during our next conference.

Again, I stand ready to assist you in making this school year a successful teaching experience.

Sincerely,

_____
Principal

Enclosure

Sample Document 4.3
Peer Observation Form

PEER OBSERVATION FORM

_____ School

Date _____ Time of Day _____ Class Period _____
Teacher Observing _____ Teacher Teaching _____

A. Starting the School Day
    1. How did the teacher escort students to the classroom?
    2. How did the teacher greet the students?
    3. What communication took place between the teacher and students?
    4. What opening school day activities occurred in the classroom? Were they planned or on-the-spot decisions? Were the activities work or fun? Was a time limit set?
    5. How did the teacher take attendance? (Using the seating chart? By homework turned in? Other?)
    6. How did the teacher collect money (lunch/supply/field trip)?

B. Classroom Instruction
    1. Did the teacher begin the lesson with a motivational activity to capture students' attention?
    2. Did the teacher make the objective known to students?
    3. How was the instructional material presented?
    4. How did the teacher begin the lesson quickly?
    5. What was the level of student participation?
    6. How did the teacher keep the students motivated during the lesson?
    7. How did the teacher use good examples?
    8. How did the teacher use a variety of questions?
    9. How mobile was the teacher? Did the teacher stand in one location or move around?
    10. Did the teacher's position affect discipline?

C. Lesson Closure
    1. How did the teacher close the lesson?
    2. How was completed work collected?
    3. How did the teacher assign homework?

D. Classroom management
    1. What were the teacher's classroom management plans?

     2. What classroom management strategies were used to operate the classroom?

     3. What features reflected the teacher's enthusiasm (i.e., vocal delivery, eye movement, gestures, body movement, facial expression, word selection, acceptance of ideas and feelings, and overall energy)?

E. Observation Conclusions
     1. How did the teacher end the lesson?
     2. How do you think the lesson went?
     3. Did learning take place? How do you know?
     4. Was discipline a problem?
     5. What strategies did the teacher use that could help you improve your teaching?
     6. What worked well? What did not work well?
     7. What insights have you gained from observing this teacher?

Sample Document 4.4
Letter Confirming Arrangements for the Teacher
to Shadow a Teacher in Another School
(Place on school letterhead)

Date

Name of Teacher
School Address

Dear _____:

As we have discussed earlier, opportunities are available for teachers to observe classes in other schools in our district. Therefore I have made arrangements for you to spend an entire day at _____ School, which is located at _____ .

You are to report to the school office to meet with the principal, _____ , at _____ A.M. on _____ , 20XX. You will spend the entire day in the _____ grade classroom of _____ .

_____ is an experienced teacher who has excellent classroom management skills as well as fine instructional techniques. If you believe it would be worthwhile, I can also arrange to have _____ visit your classroom.

Again, I stand ready to assist you in making this school year a successful teaching experience.

Sincerely,

_____
Principal

Sample Document 4.5
Letter Confirming Arrangements to Have a Teacher From Another School Visit the Teacher's Classroom
(Place on school letterhead)

Date

Name of Teacher
School Address

Dear _____:

I was pleased that your visit to _____ School was a worthwhile professional development experience for you. Because I want to continue assisting you in improving your teaching performance, I have made arrangements for _____, a _____ grade teacher from _____, to spend the entire school day in your classroom on _____. During that time, _____ will work with you in the following areas:

> (List specific areas, e.g., classroom management, reading instruction, general organizational rules, procedures, routines, instructional strategies.)

Again, I stand ready to assist you in making this school year a successful teaching experience.

Sincerely,

_____
Principal

Sample Document 4.6
*Letter Referring the Teacher to Specific Sections
in the Teachers' Handbook*
(Place on school letterhead)

Date

Name of Teacher
School Address

Dear _____ :

At the beginning of the school year, you received a copy of The _____
School Teachers' Handbook. This handbook is designed to provide information
that will clarify rules and procedures for ensuring the smooth operation of the
school. Please review the following sections:

Section	Title
•	
•	
•	

I stand ready to assist you in making this a successful school year.

Sincerely,

_____

Principal

Enclosures

(NOTE: Include a copy of the pages cited in the handbook or the table of contents when preparing the Unsatisfactory Teacher Evaluation Document.)

Sample Document 4.7
Letter Referring the Teacher to WWW Sites
(Place on school letterhead)

Date

Name of Teacher
School Address

Dear _____:

As you know, our school is connected to the Internet through the school district's Technology Department. Several World Wide Web (WWW) sites that are available for teachers are listed in the enclosed brochure. I would like you to explore the following web sites dealing with effective teaching strategies:

-
-
-

I have heard many positive comments from teachers about these Web sites and believe they contain information that will help you improve your teaching.

I stand ready to assist you in making this a successful school year.

Sincerely,

_____
Principal

Enclosure

Sample Document 4.8
Letter Providing Videotapes on Classroom Management/Instructional Strategies
(Place on school letterhead)

Date

Name of Teacher
School Address

Dear _____:

I am providing you with a copy of the following videotapes that show successful classroom management techniques and instructional strategies:

-
-
-

I would like you to review these tapes and then meet with me to discuss the incorporation of these techniques into your classroom management plan with the intent of improving your teaching performance.

Please see my secretary to schedule a meeting with me.

Sincerely,

_____
Principal

Enclosures

Sample Document 4.9
Letter Requesting Clarification Relative
to the Teacher's Classroom Procedures
(Place on school letterhead)

Date

Name of Teacher
School Address

Dear _____:

This is the fifth week of the school year, and I am concerned about what appears to be a lack of procedures in your classroom. When I observed your classroom yesterday, I was uncertain that students knew your procedures. Please take time to describe your procedures for the following basic classroom activities:

A. Beginning Class
    1. Taking and recording attendance and tardiness
    2. Providing academic warm-ups
    3. Distributing materials
    4. Beginning the lesson
    5. Gaining students' attention

B. Use of Classroom and School Areas
    1. Drinks, bathroom, pencil sharpener
    2. Student storage
    3. Learning centers
    4. Playground and school grounds

C. Work Requirements and Procedures
    1. Paper heading
    2. Use of pen or pencil
    3. Writing on the back of paper
    4. Neatness and legibility
    5. Incomplete work
    6. Late work
    7. Missed work
    8. Independent work
    9. Definition of "working alone"
    10. Passing out books and supplies
    11. Movement in and out of small groups

12. Expected behavior in groups
13. Out-of-seat policies
14. Talking among students (general and during seatwork)
15. Conduct during interruptions
16. Homework assignments
17. Collecting assignments
18. Marking/grading papers
19. Returning assignments
20. Posting student work
21. Rewards and incentives

Plan to complete your response and forward it to me by _____, 20XX.

Sincerely,

_____

Principal

Sample Document 4.10
Letter Identifying Articles on Classroom Management
(Place on school letterhead)

Date

Name of Teacher
School Address

Dear _____:

Enclosed you will find a copy of the following articles that I believe will help you improve your classroom management and teaching techniques:

-
-
-
-

In closing, I stand ready to assist you in making this school year a successful teaching experience.

Sincerely,

_____

Principal

Enclosures

(NOTE: Include a copy of the articles when preparing the Unsatisfactory Teacher Evaluation Document.)

Sample Document 4.11
Letter Providing a Book Publisher Catalog
(Place on school letterhead)

Date

Name of Teacher
School Address

Dear _____:

Enclosed is a copy of the 20XX-20XX catalog from the _____ Publishing Company. All classroom teachers are allocated funds to purchase supplies and books; you may want to use a portion of these funds to order some reference books that will help you improve your teaching.

If you are interested in purchasing any of these books, please follow the ordering procedures outlined in the teachers' handbook.

Sincerely,

_____
Principal

Enclosure

Sample Document 4.12
Letter Referring the Teacher to the Weekly Bulletin
(Place on school letterhead)

Date

Name of Teacher
School Address

Dear _____:

As you know, the weekly staff bulletin is distributed at the end of the day on Fridays. It is printed on goldenrod paper so that it easily stands out from other papers and staff members know that it is important to read.

The bulletin contains information about daily school events for the next week and also has a monthly schedule of upcoming school activities. In addition to listing these events and activities, detailed information is provided, including the responsibilities of staff members at these activities.

The sections of the weekly bulletin are Good News Celebration, Daily Activities, Staff Checklist, and Looking Ahead. The tips in the checklist are suggestions for running an effective school (e.g., teachers are reminded to pick up their students on time and quietly escort them to their classrooms).

I want you to reread the Staff Checklist section in the weekly bulletins that have been distributed to date and continue to read future weekly bulletins throughout the remainder of the school year. This is valuable information that can help you improve your teaching performance.

Sincerely,

_____

Principal

Enclosures

(NOTE: Include a copy of the weekly bulletins when preparing the Unsatisfactory Teacher Evaluation Document.)

Sample Document 4.13
Letter Encouraging the Teacher to Attend
Workshops or Classes
(Place on school letterhead)

Date

Name of Teacher
School Address

Dear _____:

The _____ School District Staff Bulletin lists several inservice classes that should be beneficial in improving your classroom teaching performance. I suggest that you enroll in the following class(es):

-
-
-

Registration forms are available in the school office.

As always, I stand ready to assist you in making this school year a successful teaching experience.

Sincerely,

_____
Principal

(NOTE: Include a copy of the pages from the bulletin when preparing the Unsatisfactory Teacher Evaluation Document.)

Sample Document 4.14
Letter Encouraging the Teacher to Attend a Convention
(Place on school letterhead)

Date

Name of Teacher
School Address

Dear _____:

The _____ Teachers' Convention is scheduled to be held from _____, 20XX, to _____, 20XX, at _____ (specific location). The convention booklet lists several workshops that should assist you in improving your teaching performance. I suggest that you register and attend the following workshops:

Title	Date	Time	Room

As always, I stand ready to assist you in making this school year a successful teaching experience.

Sincerely,

_____
Principal

Sample Document 4.15
Letter Summarizing a Meeting Held With the Teacher
(Place on school letterhead)

Date

Name of Teacher
School Address

Dear _____:

This letter serves as a summary of our meeting, which was held in my office on
_____ at _____ A.M./P.M. I began the meeting by stating my concerns about your inability to effectively manage your classroom. My concerns
were as follows:

    1.

    2.

    3.

We also discussed the support materials and opportunities that were provided
for you. In addition, I gave you the following suggestions to improve your classroom management skills:

    1.

    2.

    3.

I want to continue supporting your efforts to improve your classroom management
skills and stand ready to assist you in improving your teaching effectiveness.

Sincerely,

_____
Principal

Sample Document 4.16
Letter Reviewing Assistance Provided to the Teacher
(Place on school letterhead)

Date

Name of Teacher
School Address

Dear _____:

During the past ___ weeks, I have made suggestions to help you improve your teaching performance in the following areas:

-
-
-
-

I would like to meet with you to discuss these suggestions for improvement and the progress that you have made. Please contact my secretary to schedule an appointment with me. As always, I stand ready to assist you in making this school year a successful teaching experience.

Sincerely,

_____
Principal

Sample Document 4.17
Memorandum to the Principal's Supervisor
Summarizing Observations, Conferences,
and Support Provided to the Teacher
(Place on school letterhead)

DATE:
TO:
FROM:
RE: Potential Unsatisfactory Evaluation

During September and October 20XX, formal and informal observations were conducted in all teachers' classrooms. I observed _____ on

Day _____   Date _____   Time _____

(List day, dates and times.)

These observations represent a reasonable sampling and included_____ _____'s assignment, morning and afternoon.

During postobservation conferences, _____'s strengths and weaknesses were discussed. In addition, I offered suggestions for improvement, discussed assistance available, and set a reasonable period of time for necessary improvement.

Enclosed is a copy of the summary letter that was given to _____ on _____ offering specific suggestions for improvement. Also enclosed are copies of the formal and informal observation/evaluation forms used to observe _____.

I have used the same formal and informal observation/evaluation forms that were presented to all teachers on September _____, 20XX, with a letter explaining the evaluation process at _____ School. I will keep you informed regarding the issuance of this potential unsatisfactory teacher evaluation and would like for you to review my documentation before it is finalized.

cc: Attorney for the school district

Enclosures

Sample Document 4.18
Cover Page for the Unsatisfactory
Teacher Evaluation Documentation
(Place on school letterhead)

UNSATISFACTORY TEACHER EVALUATION DOCUMENTATION

for

_____

SUBMITTED BY

_____, PRINCIPAL

_____ SCHOOL

_____ _____, 20XX

Sample Document 4.19
Table of Contents for the Unsatisfactory Teacher Evaluation Documentation

Begin to organize the unsatisfactory teacher evaluation documentation into a format similar to the sample format (such as the basic outline provided in the following table of contents) and place it in a three-ring binder (two or more inches thick). It is important that your documentation as well as your presentation is in a logical sequence for you to present and for a hearing officer at any level to follow and understand.

This binder will serve as the master document, which should be kept in a locked school cabinet. The master document should not be saved on any hard drives at school but rather saved on an original disk and a back-up disk.

Prior to the initial unsatisfactory evaluation conference, make any additional copies that you will need. For example, the teacher's representative should receive a binder with all of the documentation—except your opening and closing statements and any personal notes that you might have (Lawrence & Vachon, 1997, p. 60).

CONTENTS

   I. Letters to Staff Members at the Beginning of School
      A. Welcome Staff to the School
      B. Identification of a Mentor Teacher

   II. Identification of Evaluator
      A. Letter Identifying the Teacher's Evaluator
      B. School Roster for Teachers' Initials Acknowledging Receipt of Evaluation Letter

   III. Observation/Evaluation Procedures for the School
      A. Letter Explaining the Evaluation Process
      B. Informal Observation/Evaluation Form
      C. Formal Observation/Evaluation Form

   IV. Observation Documentation
      A. Summaries of Monthly Observations of Staff Members
      B. Observations of the Teacher
      C. Summary Letters of Conferences Following Observations of the Teacher

   V. Memoranda of Concerns

VI. Letters/Documents Relative to Assistance Provided
  A. Visiting a Classroom in the Same School
  B. Peer Observation Form
  C. Shadowing by the Teacher in Another School
  D. Visitation by a Teacher From Another School
  E. Section in the Teachers' Handbook
  F. Articles to Read
  G. Workshop to Attend
  H. Convention to Attend
  I. Videotapes to View
  J. World Wide Web (WWW) Internet Sites
  K. Ordering from a Publisher's Catalog
  L. Weekly Bulletins
  M. Classroom Procedures
  N. Review of Assistance

VII. Discipline Referrals

VIII. Parental Complaints
  A. Letters Informing the Teacher About Parental Complaints
  B. Parental Complaints Filed Against the Teacher

IX. Work Samples

X. Unsatisfactory Evaluation Letters and Evaluation
  A. Memoranda to the Principal's Supervisor Summarizing Observations, Conferences, and Support Provided to the Teacher
  B. Failure to Achieve a Satisfactory Level of Performance
  C. Intent to Issue an Unsatisfactory Evaluation
  D. Meeting Reminder
  E. Unsatisfactory Evaluation

Sample Document 4.20
*Checklist for Collecting Historical Information
About the Teacher*

_____ SCHOOL

20XX–20XX

TEACHER: _____

❑ Contact the personnel department to verify the teacher's area of certification.

❑ Check the teacher's personnel file and read any previous letters warning the teacher about unsatisfactory teaching performance. Note the dates and the name(s) of the principal(s).

❑ Check the teacher's personnel file and read previous teacher evaluation documents. Carefully read for written comments about unsatisfactory teaching performance or warnings given by previous principals as well as comments providing suggestions for improvement. Note the dates and the name(s) of the principal(s).

❑ Check the local school file for any written warnings about an unsatisfactory teacher evaluation. Note the dates and the name(s) of the principal(s).

❑ Check the local school records to find out the number of days the teacher has been absent and the number of times the teacher has been late to work as related to an unsatisfactory teacher evaluation.

❑ Contact the personnel department to find out the number of days the teacher has been absent during the past three years.

❑ Check the local school file for any misconduct charges against the teacher as related to an unsatisfactory teacher evaluation.

❑ Contact the department responsible for workers' compensation to determine if the teacher has filed claims for workers' compensation as related to an unsatisfactory teacher evaluation.

Implementing a Plan for Intensive Assistance

You must provide support and assistance to help marginal teachers improve their teaching performance.

Suggested Time Line: November

Step 4 in the process of evaluating the marginal teacher involves providing intensive assistance and documenting an individualized plan that lists specific concerns, suggestions to help the teacher improve his or her performance, and specific dates when the teacher is to complete or fulfill each suggestion.

If your school district does not require a formal intensive assistance plan, you should continue to use the memorandum of concerns to document the assistance that you provided to the teacher. The format for an intensive assistance plan is shown in Sample Document 5.1. This form contains sections for background information, concerns, the teacher's plan for improvement, the principal's plan for providing assistance, comments, and the principal's final recommendation relative to continuation of the teacher's employment in the school district. Key phrases to substantiate unsatisfactory teaching performance are shown in Resource B. The intensive assistance plans should state the consequences if the teacher's performance does not improve. We want to reiterate that you must adhere to state statutes and contractual requirements that pertain to using an intensive assistance plan for the teacher.

During November, the following procedures should occur:

❏ Prior to formal observation of a teacher receiving intensive assistance, hold a preobservation conference and have the teacher discuss his or her lesson plans and expected outcomes of the lesson you will observe.

❏ Conduct *three* formal observations lasting approximately 30 minutes to 1 hour, and provide feedback that lists areas of weakness and suggestions for improvement. Give a three-week time period for the teacher to accomplish these necessary improvements.

❏ Following the observation, write a memorandum of concerns that lists suggestions for improvement, and hold a meeting to discuss the concerns (see Sample Document 4.1). During the postobservation conference, begin the meeting by stating what the teacher did well and then discuss the areas that need improvement.

❏ Write a letter to the teacher summarizing the meeting held to discuss concerns and suggestions (see Sample Document 4.15).

❏ Continue conducting daily observations to identify teachers who may be experiencing classroom problems and maintain the Summary Form for Formal and Informal Classroom Observations (see Sample Document 3.6).

❏ Provide opportunities for the teacher to attend workshops conducted by the school district (see Sample Document 4.13).

❏ Provide the teacher with videotapes that show proper classroom management strategies and instructional techniques (see Sample Documents 4.8).

❏ Videotape or audiotape the teacher's class and then meet to discuss the tape.

❏ Offer the teacher articles to read that include suggestions for improvement in classroom management and instructional strategies (see Sample Document 4.10).

❏ Issue a letter reviewing assistance provided to the teacher (see Sample Document 4.16).

❏ Send a potential unsatisfactory evaluation update letter to your supervisor (see Sample Document 4.17).

❏ Continue maintaining a parental complaint file (for both verbal and written complaints) for each teacher (see Sample Documents 3.7 and 3.8).

❏ Continue collecting samples of assignments that the teacher gives to students to make sure that they conform to district standards. Retain these samples in the teacher's file.

❏ If the quality of work samples is poor, write another memorandum of concerns to the teacher and offer suggestions for improvement (see Sample 4.1).

❑ Continue monitoring the quantity of busywork (e.g., photocopies) that teachers give to the students.

❑ Continue keeping a record of the number of pending suspensions, suspension letters sent to parents, and other disciplinary actions taken by the teacher.

❑ Continue keeping copies of all notes the teacher writes to you about his or her discipline problems or other school-related issues.

❑ Maintain contact with the district's personnel department representative and attorney.

❑ Check to see if the teacher enrolled in and attended the suggested workshop or classes.

❑ Have your assistant principal conduct daily informal observations. Give the teacher a copy of the actual observation form and keep a file copy.

❑ Continue using the weekly school bulletin to provide teaching techniques, classroom management strategies, and other information to document your attempt to give assistance to the teaching staff.

❑ If support services are available from central administration, submit a request for a staff member to observe the teacher's classroom.

❑ Continue recording each parental complaint on the standard complaint form, and meet with the teacher about the situation. Write your disposition on the parental complaint form and forward it to the teacher for his or her response. File both copies.

❑ Continue recording the number of students referred to the office for disrupting the class with date, time, reason, the teacher's comments, the teacher's recommendation, and the administrative disposition (see Sample Document 3.9).

❑ Take pictures in the classroom, particularly if the teacher is experiencing classroom management problems.

Sample Document 5.1
Intensive Assistance Plan

INTENSIVE ASSISTANCE PLAN
_____ SCHOOL DISTRICT

Name _____ Date _____
Date Plan Initiated _____ Date Plan Completed _____
Assignment _____ School Site _____

   I. List of Concerns
      A.
      B.
      C.
      D.
      E.
      F.
      G.
      H.
      I.
      J.

  II. Teacher's Plan for Improvement
      A.
      B.
      C.
      D.
      E.
      F.
      G.
      H.
      I.
      J.

 III. Plans to Assist Teacher
      A.
      B.
      C.
      D.
      E.
      F.
      G.
      H.
      I.
      J.

IV. Evaluator's Comments (check one)

____ Has met the expectation and time lines of the intensive assistance plan.

____ Has not met the expectation and timeliness of the intensive assistance plan.

V. Final Recommendations

____ Recommend continuing employment, discontinuing intensive assistance.

____ Recommend continuing employment, continuing intensive assistance.

____ Recommend starting dismissal procedures.

Teacher's Signature _____ Date _____

Principal's Signature _____ Date _____

Supervisor's Signature _____ Date _____

Note to Teacher: Your signature acknowledges that you are aware of your intensive assistance plan. It does not mean that you concur with the plan.

cc: Chief Personnel Director
    Teacher
    Teacher's Representative

6 Deciding on Retention or Dismissal

When making the tough decision, you must keep the educational rights of the children foremost in your thoughts.

Suggested Time Line: December

Step 5 in the process of evaluating the marginal teacher is to make a determination as to whether the teacher should be retained or dismissed. If you believe that the teacher should be dismissed, prepare to send the potential unsatisfactory evaluation letter to the teacher. During this time, you should continue to conduct informal and formal classroom observations of all teachers. During December, the teacher(s) identified to receive the unsatisfactory evaluation should be formally observed *three* times. You can conduct informal observations on a weekly basis. To meet the deadline for informing the teacher of the potential unsatisfactory evaluation, it is critical that you adhere to this time line.

During December, the following procedures should occur:

❏ Prior to formal observations of teachers receiving intensive assistance, hold a preobservation conference with each one and have the teacher discuss his or her lesson plan and expected outcomes of the lesson you will observe.

❏ Conduct *three* formal observations and provide feedback listing areas of weakness and recommendations for improvement and reiterate the time line of expected improvement.

❑ Following observations, write a memorandum of concerns that lists suggestions for improvements and hold a meeting to discuss the concerns (see Sample Document 4.1).

❑ Continue conducting daily observations to identify teachers who may be experiencing classroom problems.

❑ Continue providing articles for the teacher to read (see Sample Document 4.10).

❑ Continue providing teaching tips in the weekly staff bulletin.

❑ Continue maintaining the parental complaint file (see Sample Documents 3.7 and 3.8).

❑ Continue collecting samples of assignments that teachers give to students to make sure they conform to district standards. Retain these samples in each teacher's file.

❑ If the quality of work samples is poor, write another memorandum of concerns to the teacher and offer suggestions for improvement (see Sample Document 4.1).

❑ Continue keeping a record of the number of pending suspensions, suspension letters sent to parents, and other disciplinary actions of the teacher.

❑ Continue keeping copies of all notes written to you by the teacher about his or her discipline problems or other school-related issues.

❑ Maintain contact with the district's personnel department representative and attorney for the district.

❑ Issue a letter to the teacher stating the possibility of an unsatisfactory evaluation if he or she fails to achieve a satisfactory level of teaching performance (see Sample Document 6.1).

❑ Send an update letter about the potential unsatisfactory evaluation to your supervisor (see Sample Document 4.17).

❑ Hand deliver the letter regarding the possibility of an unsatisfactory evaluation on a Friday afternoon.

❑ Work in collaboration with the assistant principal or central administration staff members who can conduct teacher evaluations.

Sample Document 6.1
Letter Stating the Possibility of an Unsatisfactory Evaluation
(Place on school letterhead)

Date

Name of Teacher
School Address

Dear _____ :

Beginning in September and continuing through December of the 20XX-20XX school year, formal and informal observations were conducted of your classroom. Specifically, I observed you on

Day	Date	Time

These observations represented a reasonable sampling of your teaching performance and included all aspects of your assignment, morning and afternoon.

In addition to memoranda that were sent to you outlining my concerns, I held conferences with you to discuss deficiencies, available assistance, and suggestions for improvement, as well as set a reasonable time for necessary improvement. On_____, _____, and _____, I sent you letters that summarized our conferences.

Unfortunately, at this time, your teaching performance has not improved to a satisfactory level. Therefore this letter serves as official notification that failure to achieve a satisfactory level of achievement by January _____, 20XX, will result in the issuance of an unsatisfactory evaluation with a recommendation for your dismissal from the _____ School District.

Sincerely,

_____
Principal

7

Following Through With the Dismissal Process

Don't fear the process of removing a marginal teacher from the classroom.

Suggested Time Line: January

Step 6 of the teacher dismissal process will probably be the most emotionally challenging experience for you because that is when you decide to follow through with issuing the unsatisfactory teacher evaluation. If you decide to proceed, you must start preparing the documentation needed for the formal unsatisfactory evaluation proceedings and reviewing strategies for conducting the unsatisfactory evaluation conference with the teacher and the teacher's representative(s). Carefully selected wording is essential. Examples of key phrases are provided in Resource B. The teacher should have no surprises at the meetings and hearings. The procedures in this step ensure that you followed due process as well as met the guidelines of the teachers' bargaining unit, school board policies, state statutes, and federal laws.

During January, the following procedures should occur:

❏ Continue conducting formal and informal classroom observations and conferences as necessary.

❏ Draft the letter of intent to issue an unsatisfactory evaluation, and hand deliver it to the teacher on a Friday afternoon, with a copy to the bargaining unit (see Sample Document 7.1).

❏ Prepare the opening and closing statements for the unsatisfactory evaluation meeting and include reference to just cause (see Sample Documents 7.2 and 7.3).

❏ Review the unsatisfactory evaluation binder to ensure that all appropriate documentation is included.

❏ Maintain contact with the district's personnel department representative and the attorney for the district.

❏ Meet with your supervisor to discuss your unsatisfactory evaluation documentation.

❏ Draft the unsatisfactory evaluation using the established form for your district (see Sample Document 7.4).

❏ Send a letter to the teacher to remind the teacher about the date, time, and location of the meeting (see Sample Document 7.5).

❏ Prepare additional copies of the unsatisfactory evaluation binder (one for the teacher, one for the teacher's representative, one for the district representative who will conduct the unsatisfactory teacher evaluation conference, and one for yourself).

❏ Prepare for the conference and the cross-examination (e.g., be knowledgeable of questions that might be asked by the teacher's legal adviser, prepare to respond to questions or criticisms regarding how you conducted the evaluation process).

❏ See Resource C for specific suggestions.

❏ Conduct the unsatisfactory evaluation meeting, incorporating these nine steps:

1. Have an assistant principal or another administrative staff member who has participated in the evaluation process attend the meeting to take notes.
2. Determine the best seating position at the conference (e.g., do not sit between the teacher and his or her representative). Instead, sit at the head of the table or behind the desk (see Sample Document 7.6; Lawrence & Vachon, 1997, p. 95).
3. Greet individuals attending the conference and establish guidelines for the proceedings (see Sample Document 7.7; Lawrence & Vachon, 1997, pp. 96–97).
4. If the teacher brings an attorney and a union representative, request that the teacher's official representative be identified before proceeding with the conference. The other individual(s) can only observe.
5. Have a copy of the teachers' contract on the desk or table.

6. Maintain a formal atmosphere.

7. Read the opening statement.

8. Distribute the binders.

9. Present all evidence to substantiate the unsatisfactory evaluation at the first meeting. New evidence may not be presented at subsequent hearings.

Sample Document 7.1
Letter of Intent to Issue an Unsatisfactory Evaluation
(Place on school letterhead)

Date

Name of Teacher
School Address

Dear _____:

This letter is to inform you that I plan to submit an unsatisfactory teacher evaluation for you to the Department of School Personnel. I will give you a copy of this evaluation on _____, 20XX, at _____ P.M. in my office.

The Master Contract, Part ___, Section ___, on pages _____, governs the due process of teacher performance evaluations. If you wish, you may be represented by a member of your bargaining unit or other person of your choice.

After the conference, you will be allowed ___ hours to study my comments and respond to them in writing. The unsatisfactory evaluation will then be filed with the Department of School Personnel with a recommendation for your dismissal from the _____ School District.

Sincerely,

_____
Principal

Sample Document 7.2
Opening Statement for the
Unsatisfactory Evaluation Conference

An unsatisfactory evaluation is issued when a teacher fails to respond to the efforts that were made to help improve his or her teaching performance and his or her failure to develop a behavioral management plan to reduce negative student behaviors. When this occurs, poor teaching performance and a lack of an effective student behavioral management plan have a negative impact on students.

Prior to issuance of this unsatisfactory evaluation, contractual procedures were followed to ensure that procedural and substantive due process were applied. Part ___, Section ___, on page _____ of the contract identifies the steps that are required by the _____ School District.

_____ has been a teacher in the _____ School District since _____, working at _____ and _____ Schools. He/She was evaluated by _____ during the 20XX-20XX school year and by _____ during the 20XX-20XX school year. Both of his/her supervisors found his/her teaching skills to be below average. During those two separate assignments in two different schools, he/she was unable to reach and maintain a level of acceptable teaching performance.

_____ is licensed in _____ and holds certification to work in the capacity of a teacher at _____ grade levels in _____ subject area(s).

The following letters are on file in _____'s employee file in the personnel department regarding his/her unsatisfactory teaching performance:

Date	Principal	Summary of Statements Regarding Performance
•		
•		
•		

The following unsatisfactory evaluations are on file in _____'s employee file in the personnel department warning him/her about unsatisfactory teaching performance:

Date	Principal	Summary of Statements Regarding Performance

•

•

•

Listed to follow is a summary of _____ 's absenteeism during the past three years:

Year	Number of Days Absent	Total Hours Absent
20XX-20XX		
20XX-20XX		
20XX-20XX		

On different occasions, _____ filed for workers' compensation related to teaching performance:

Year	Claim	Disposition
20XX		
20XX		
20XX		

During his/her assignment at _____ School, he/she has been

Absent _____ times for a total of _____ hours:

Dates	Number of Hours	Reasons

Late to work _____ times for a total of _____ hours:

Dates	Number of Hours	Reasons

Charged with the following actions of misconduct related to teaching performance:

Dates	Charge	Disposition

Parents have also called the principal and written letters about the conditions in _____ 's classroom:

Just-Cause Requirements

The teacher evaluation process for the school and school district was made known to all teachers in the school and the process was consistently followed:

_____ was not singled out, and the same standards were applied to all teachers.

Observations of _____ included all phases of his/her assignments.

A continuous and accurately dated file of all observations and evaluations was maintained.

_____ received written memoranda of concerns specifying the exact nature of the teaching deficiencies.

_____ received specific suggestions in memoranda of concerns for correcting these teaching deficiencies and how to achieve a satisfactory level of teaching performance.

_____ was given a reasonable period of time for necessary improvements.

_____ was informed that failure to achieve an acceptable level of teaching performance by (date) _____ would result in the issuance of an unsatisfactory evaluation.

Despite the opportunities for self-improvement prior to issuing this unsatisfactory evaluation, _____ did not attain or maintain an acceptable level of teaching performance.

In closing, _____'s overall teaching performance is related to undesirable student behaviors. Moreover, _____ failed to respond to the efforts that were made to help improve his/her teaching performance, and he/she failed to develop a behavioral management plan to reduce negative student behavior. These are justifications for issuing an unsatisfactory teacher evaluation.

At this point, I will provide these binders containing the documentation to support the unsatisfactory evaluation that has been issued to _____.

(NOTE: This opening statement should not be included in the Unsatisfactory Teacher Evaluation Document. It should be read at the beginning of each hearing.)

Sample Document 7.3
Closing Statement for the
Unsatisfactory Evaluation Conference

Unfortunately, _____'s overall teaching performance is related to undesirable student behaviors. _____ failed to respond to the efforts that were made to help improve his/her teaching performance and he/she failed to develop a behavioral management plan to reduce negative student behavior. These are justifications for issuing an unsatisfactory teacher evaluation.

Therefore I am recommending that _____ be relieved of his/her teaching responsibilities at _____ School and that he/she be terminated from the _____ School District, effective at the end of the 20XX-20XX school year.

(NOTE: This closing statement should not be included in the Unsatisfactory Teacher Evaluation Document. It should be read at the end of each hearing.)

Sample Document 7.4
Evaluation Form

TEACHER PERFORMANCE EVALUATION

DATE _____

NAME _____   SUBJECT/GRADES _____

SCHOOL _____   YEAR 20XX-20XX

(NOTE: Use the individual district evaluation form and include specific reasons why the teacher failed to meet standards of the profession.)

Principals and other personnel delegated by position or assignment to evaluate the performance of the teacher are requested to complete the evaluation form. In the space provided, include a statement that supports the assessment.

In my professional judgment, _____ is not making a satisfactory contribution to the educational program at _____ School. Although he/she has exhibited some positive characteristics, _____ has failed to meet the standards of the profession. It is recommended that he/she be dismissed from the school district next semester for the following reasons:

1.
2.
3.
4.
5.

_____   _____
Evaluator   Principal

Sample Document 7.5
Letter Reminding the Teacher About the
Unsatisfactory Evaluation Meeting
(Place on School Letterhead)

Date

Name of Teacher
School Address

Dear _____:

This letter is to remind you about our meeting, which is scheduled for _____, 20XX, at _____ in my office. The purpose of this meeting is to discuss the issuance of an unsatisfactory teacher evaluation to you.

If you wish, you may be represented by a bargaining unit representative or anyone of your choice.

Sincerely,

_____
Principal

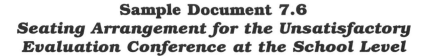

Sample Document 7.6
Seating Arrangement for the Unsatisfactory
Evaluation Conference at the School Level

SCHOOL-LEVEL CONFERENCE SEATING ARRANGEMENT

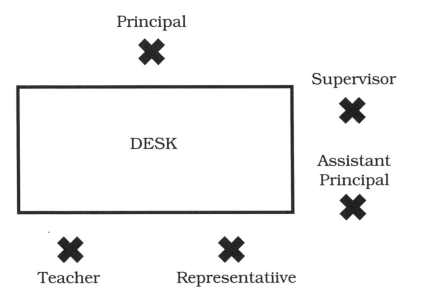

This seating chart shows one possible arrangement for the school-level confer-ence. As the principal, you are in charge of the hearing. Therefore you must clar-ify procedures, set basic ground rules, and explain the sequence of the hearing. You should formally greet the teacher and the teacher's representative and intro-duce the teacher's supervisor and the assistant principal in attendance at the conference. The role of the assistant principal is to take notes of the meeting. He or she does not play an active role in this conference. You should have a copy of the master contract on the table or desk in front of you and refer to the section of the contract that governs the evaluation process. The primary speakers are the principal, the teacher's representative, and the supervisor. The assistant principal may make a pertinent statement relative to his or her role in any obser-vations and assistance provided to the teacher as well as respond to any ques-tions from the teacher's representative. The teacher's representative may do all of the talking for the teacher or may ask the teacher to respond to questions or make a statement.

Sample Document 7.7
Greeting and Guidelines for the School-Level Conference

Greeting	"Good afternoon, Mr./Ms. _____."
Introductions if you do not know the teacher representative	"My name is _____. I am the principal of _____ School. Mr./Ms. _____ is the _____ supervisor who has also worked with Mr./Ms. _____. Mr./Ms. _____, assistant principal will sit in on the conference to take notes."
Acknowledgment of contractual provision and due process	"As I stated in my letter to you, the meeting today is to issue an unsatisfactory evaluation in accordance with Section _____, Paragraph _____ of the master contract. You will be given _____ hours to review the evaluation, sign it, and return it to me no later than _____. If you wish, you may attach a response to your evaluation, and they will both be sent to the personnel department."
Sequence of testimony	"As we proceed, I will present documentation to support the unsatisfactory evaluation. I would like to proceed without interruptions, and I will also call on Mr./Ms. _____ to provide documentation relative to his/her observations, support, and assessment of Mr./Ms. _____'s performance. After we have finished, Mr./Ms. _____, you and your representative will have an opportunity to examine the documentation and provide testimony."
Clarification of procedure	"Do you have any questions about the procedures for this conference? Let's proceed with the conference."

Remember that if the teacher brings more than one person to the conference, you should ask the teacher to identify one person to serve as his/her official representative before proceeding with the meeting. Any other individuals can only observe. Do not allow notes to be passed between the teacher or others attending the meeting. Most important, do not allow audio or video taping of the conference.

8 Preparing for the Third-Party Hearing and Bringing Closure

If the teacher's representative begins to attack you personally rather than attacking your documentation of the teacher, you have done a good job preparing the documentation.

Suggested Time Line: February — June

Step 7 is one of the most challenging steps in the process because you will be presenting your case at a third-party hearing where the hearing officer will determine if your documentation substantiates the dismissal. This step continues the due-process requirement and provides the teacher with an opportunity to present his or her side of the case. In addition, you must continue making formal and informal classroom observations.

Part of your goal in the dismissal process is to maintain a professional demeanor at all times. You must resist any temptation to discuss the process with other teachers (particularly teachers in the building where the dismissal process is occurring). An innocent comment repeated out of context can jeopardize the entire process. As a rule, personnel matters should be considered confidential issues between the administrator and the respective staff member.

During February, the following procedures should occur:

❏ Continue conducting formal and informal classroom observations.

❏ Continue providing teaching tips in the weekly staff bulletin.

❏ Prepare for presenting the unsatisfactory evaluation documentation at the next level(s).

❏ Maintain contact with the district's personnel department representative and attorney for the school district.

❏ Review the protocol for the future hearings (see Sample Document 8.1 and 8.2) (Lawrence & Vachon, 1997, pp. 105, 111).

You must continue making formal and informal classroom observations and begin preparing evaluations for all other teachers. This step shows that the evaluation process was conducted consistently and that no one teacher was singled out. It also meets the district requirements for teacher evaluations.

During March, the following procedures should occur:

❏ Continue conducting formal and informal classroom observations and conferences as necessary.

❏ Begin preparing evaluations for all other teachers.

❏ Continue providing teaching tips in the weekly staff bulletin.

❏ Maintain contact with the district's personnel department representative and the attorney for the school district.

The majority of the evaluation process has been finalized for the school year, and you can begin making preparations for bringing closure to the school year. The total evaluation process includes all staff, and completing year-end activities reinforces that fact.

During April, the following procedures should occur:

❏ Begin preparing for closing the school year.

❏ Finalize teacher evaluation documentation.

❏ Follow contractual guidelines for informing teachers about their evaluations.

During the final step in the evaluation process, you should meet with teachers to discuss their evaluations and submit the evaluation forms to central administration. This step brings closure to the evaluation process for the school year, and beginning to prepare for the next year reinforces the fact that the process is cyclical.

During May and June, the following procedures should occur:

❏ Meet individually with teachers who request further clarification about their strengths and recommendations for improvement.

❏ Complete the appropriate district forms for all teachers identified for annual evaluations.

❏ Photocopy the completed evaluation forms for the local school files and then forward the original to the district personnel department.

❏ Issue the closing school bulletin.

❏ As a method for identifying potential mentor teachers and determining staff development needs for the next school year, summarize the strengths and areas of need of the teaching staff (see Sample Document 8.3).

❏ Review the evaluation process, and modify procedures and materials as needed for the next school year.

❏ Send a letter to mentor teachers thanking them for providing support to new teachers (see Sample Document 8.4).

Sample Document 8.1
Seating Arrangement for the Unsatisfactory Evaluation Conference at the District Level

DISTRICT-LEVEL CONFERENCE SEATING ARRANGEMENT

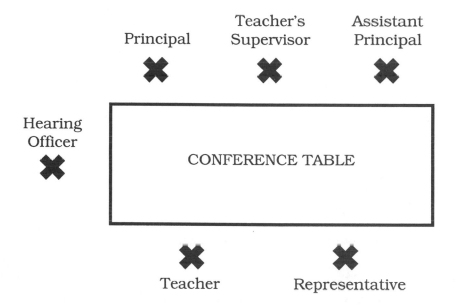

The seating arrangement shown should be used for a conference on an unsatisfactory evaluation that is held before an impartial hearing officer. The hearing officer who is in charge of this hearing makes an opening statement, usually explaining how the hearing will proceed and giving the guidelines. Both sides present their statements to the hearing officer. First, the principal presents for the administration, and the teacher's representative presents for the teacher. When you make your presentation to the hearing officer, always speak directly to him or her. Your goal is to convince the hearing officer that your documentation will substantiate the unsatisfactory evaluation. You are not trying to convince the teacher and his or her representative about the teacher's incompetence. Rather, you must convince the hearing officer—who has had no involvement in the case—that the teacher is incompetent. Therefore you must take your time to carefully explain your documentation to the hearing officer. As you speak to the hearing officer, you must make eye contact with him or her. Try not to allow the teacher and his or her representative to distract you. They may not be looking at you during your presentation. Instead, they will probably be looking at the hearing officer or taking notes on your presentation. The hearing officer may ask questions of the teacher and/or the teacher's supervisor.

Sample Document 8.2
Seating Arrangement for the Board-Level Hearing

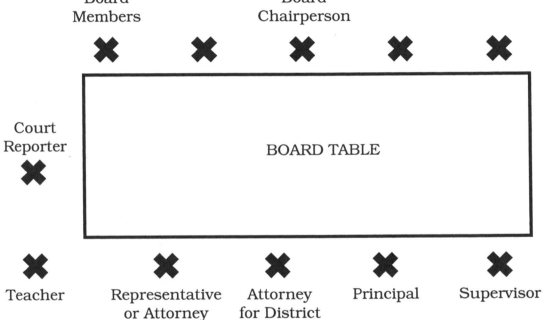

This diagram shows a general seating arrangement for a board-level hearing. Notice that the teacher and his or her representative(s) are seated together and that the principal, assistant principal, and supervisor are seated next to the attorney for the district. The board chairperson is in control of the hearing and will communicate primarily with the attorney for the district and with the teacher's representative or attorney. Again, direct your presentation to and respond to any questions from the board chairperson or individual board members. The board has separate legal counsel who may conduct the hearing. In some cases, witnesses are sequestered; however, the teacher attends throughout the hearing.

Sample Document 8.3
Chart Summarizing the Strengths and Areas of Need of the Teaching Staff

_____ School
Summary of Strengths and Areas of Need of Teaching Staff
20XX-20XX

Staff Member	Classroom Management	Classroom Instruction	Lesson Planning	High Student Expectations

Sample Document 8.4
Thank-You Letter to Mentor Teachers
(Place on school letterhead)

Date

Name of Teacher
School Address

Dear _____:

Thank you for serving as a mentor teacher for _____, a new
teacher at _____ School this school year. Sharing your ideas
and expertise about teaching has made this a rewarding and successful experience for _____.

Enclosed is a certificate of appreciation for your contributions as a teacher mentor. I hope this certificate will serve as a lasting memento of this experience.

Again, my deepest appreciation for mentoring _____ this
school year.

Sincerely,

_____
Principal

Enclosure

Key Descriptors to Use in Memoranda of Concerns

You must conduct weekly informal and formal observations/evaluations to assess the teaching performance of teachers and communicate your findings to them. If there are teaching performance problems, write a memorandum of concerns to the teacher about those problems and provide suggestions for improvement. You must accurately record the dates and times of your observations and what you observed. Also, you must clearly list your concerns about the teacher's performance and include at least one example about your concern. The following list gives examples of phrases that you can use to describe teaching performance problems.

- Caused dissension
- Failed to communicate
- Failed to have
- Did not exhibit
- Did not have
- Displayed negative

- Has an unprofessional
- Appears to lack understanding
- Proceeded without proper
- Refused to follow
- Caused friction between
- Has not maintained

- Failed to be
- Failed to produce
- Failed to improve
- Was not consistent
- Inaccurately diagnosed
- Failed to implement
- Was not authorized to
- Has been inconsistent
- Was not always prepared
- Disregarded
- Did not monitor
- Failed to follow
- Provided insufficient
- Consistently failed to
- Has made no substantial improvement
- Presented inadequate information

RESOURCE

B

Key Phrases to Substantiate Unsatisfactory Teaching Performance

To provide evidence that will support an unsatisfactory evaluation of a teacher, you must use classroom observations and teaching performance rating forms. From that documentation, you can develop statements for the unsatisfactory evaluation conferences. In the following list are phrases that you can use in describing the teacher's unsatisfactory performance:

- Failed to create an appropriate classroom atmosphere to develop the students' interest in and an attitude for learning
- Continuing pattern of unacceptable teaching practices
- Negative impact on students
- Failure to maintain classroom control
- Inability to maintain classroom control
- Inability to instruct and motivate students properly
- Failure to maintain classroom order by allowing students to randomly leave their desks without permission
- Failure to maintain classroom order by allowing students to place their feet on their desks
- Failure to create and maintain an appropriate classroom atmosphere
- Failure to effectively develop and to carry out lesson plans

- Failure to follow suggestions for remediation of ineffective teaching techniques
- Continuing pattern of unacceptable teaching practices
- Failure to respond to efforts made to assist the teacher to improve his or her teaching performance
- Failure to develop a behavioral management plan to reduce negative student behaviors
- Lack of an effective classroom management plan
- Inability to attain and maintain a level of acceptable teaching performance
- Has not achieved the acceptable level of teaching performance
- Was given a reasonable period of time for necessary improvement but has failed to improve his or her teaching performance
- Was provided with suggestions and assistance to correct deficiencies in teaching performance

C Unsatisfactory Teacher Evaluation Conferences and Hearings

You should carefully plan for the conferences and hearings that will be held to discuss the unsatisfactory evaluation and ensure that contractual time lines are met. At the school-level conference, you will conduct the meeting, present documentation, and listen to the teacher's response to the documentation. The teacher will probably, and should, bring a representative to the conference. At this conference, you, as the principal, will be the primary presenter and will call on the teacher's supervisor to present his or her testimony relative to observations and assistance. Also, if you have an assistant principal, he or she should be present to take notes. If the assistant principal also has provided documentation relative to observations and assistance, he or she may testify or respond to questions from the teacher's representative.

At the school-level conference and district-level hearing, you should not allow the use of tape recorders or video cameras. However, at the board-level hearing, a court reporter must be present, to adhere to due process required by law. Specifically, in addition to being given notification of the charges, an opportunity for a hearing, adequate time to prepare a rebuttal to the charges, access to evidence and names of witnesses, hearing before an impartial tribunal, representation by counsel, an opportunity to present evidence and witnesses, an opportunity to cross-examine adverse witnesses, and a decision based on evidence and findings of the hearing, the teacher must be provided access to a record of the hearing and an opportunity to appeal. The record of the hearing may include a court reporter transcript.

Because you should hold a meeting with the teacher and his or her representative, you must establish and maintain a formal, businesslike atmosphere.

Therefore, it essential that you plan for the conference. First of all, you must set the location to ensure privacy, determine the seating arrangement, and select the best position that will enable you to control the conference. For example, you should sit at the head of the table or behind your desk. You should never sit between the teacher and his or her representative. You should have a copy of the teacher's contract on the desk in front of you for easy reference, if necessary, and to also visually reinforce that the conference is governed by the contract.

Remember that you may not be able to anticipate everything that will happen during the conference. However, you can and should try to anticipate certain things that could potentially throw you off course. For example, if the teacher brings more than one person to the conference (e.g., an attorney, a union representative, a relative), be prepared to have the teacher identify who will be his or her official representative before proceeding with the conference. Other individuals can only observe. Another example might be the teacher and the teacher's representative trying to pass notes to each other during the conference. If it becomes excessive or disruptive, inform them that they may request a recess to communicate with each other. Do not allow verbal attacks, raised voices, or finger pointing. If you find yourself in such a combative situation, warn the teacher and the representative to conduct themselves in a professional manner or you will discontinue the conference. If the unacceptable conduct continues or the meeting becomes confrontational, you can recess the meeting for 10 to 20 minutes. After the recess, if the teacher's representative continues to act unprofessionally, stand up and announce that the meeting is adjourned.

In addition to the opening statement that you have prepared for presenting the actual documentation and the closing statement when you sum up your presentation, you will need to prepare a general greeting to open the conference and set a businesslike atmosphere. The greeting should include a reference to the contractual provision for the conference as well as the guidelines for the conference (see Sample Document 7.7). Both the general greeting and the opening statement may be read or used as a guide to present information, whichever is more comfortable. In either case, you should read through it several times before the actual conference to ensure that it flows easily. Also plan to give a documentation binder (with a capacity of two or more inches) to the teacher and the teacher's representative after your opening statement. Keep in mind that you will need to present all evidence to substantiate the unsatisfactory evaluation at the first conference. New evidence may not be presented at subsequent hearings. However, information from the time of the first conference to the next conference may be entered when the hearing officer requests an update relative to improvement and assistance provided to the teacher.

If you have followed the steps and tips in this guide, you will be confident that your documentation is well organized and supports your evaluation of the teacher's job performance. You must remember to be confident, patient, and thorough in your presentation and respond to questions from the teacher's representative with facts and evidence that can be substantiated relative to job performance and its effect on students.

Depending on the volume of documentation, this conference might last four or more hours or even need to be adjourned to continue at a later date. In the case of the latter, schedule the continuation conference as soon as possible. This conference may be lengthy. However, you should keep it moving by focusing on specifics when necessary and by summarizing or highlighting whenever possible.

It is important at the first conference to thoroughly go through the documentation and to verify that the teacher received copies of all documents that are being presented. If the representative objects to the inclusion of a document, say "I have noted your objection" and move on. It is better to leave documentation in than to take it out prematurely in the process. At a subsequent conference, the hearing officer might rule to remove the document.

You must be prepared for potential criticism on the part of the teacher and his or her representative who may accuse you of failing to provide assistance, point out spelling and grammatical errors in documentation, say that you are a poor example of a principal, accuse you of favoritism to some staff members, and accuse you of exhibiting biases based on gender, race, religion, or age. No matter how frustrated or irritated you may become when the teacher and his or her representative make these accusations, do not become defensive in your responses or exhibit facial signs that reflect your irritation. The teacher's representative will design his or her cross-examination and rebuttal to challenge your decision and to cause doubt relative to your proceeding with a recommendation for dismissal.

Always expect the unexpected. And remember that, regardless of the degree of preparation, you may not be able to anticipate everything. Therefore, expect the unexpected and remain calm if something arises that you did not anticipate. If necessary, adjourn the conference for a few minutes to determine what to do or to get an answer to a question. You might make arrangements before the conference to have an adviser (attorney for the district or your supervisor) on standby should you need on-the-spot consultation.

During the evaluation hearings, you may feel that you are on trial instead of the incompetent teacher. The teacher's representative may use confrontational strategies in an effort to frustrate you. You may be accused of showing favoritism, treating staff members differently based on race and gender, failing to clarify the roles and responsibilities, or combination of these. The teacher or the teacher's representative may further charge you with one or more of the following:

- Failed to follow state law or board policy when issuing this unsatisfactory evaluation

- Did not follow the master contract to evaluate the teacher

- Did not provide oral or written communication listing specific shortcomings and recommendations for improvement

- Harassed the teacher by conducting excessive observations

- Singled out this teacher from other teachers

- Have a vendetta against the teacher

- Have overstated the problem

- Are not qualified to conduct this evaluation because of your certification

The teacher will make every attempt to embarrass you to thwart the dismissal. Therefore, as mentioned earlier, you should avoid informal social gatherings with staff members, especially those that may involve drinking, such as house parties or going to bars. Furthermore, you must never become romantically involved with a teacher or another staff member. Not only would such rumors be likely to surface during the evaluation process, but during the dismissal hearings, they might explode in the media.

Regardless of accusations that are made about how you conducted the teacher's performance evaluation, you must not show your anger or frustration. Raising your voice and shouting at the teacher and his or her representative will only encourage them to intensify their cross-examination and to continue making false accusations. Despite the fact that you will be under stress during the hearing, you must demonstrate poise, grace, and professionalism.

If you have followed the procedures in this guide, your decision will probably not change. Therefore at the conclusion of the conference, the teacher's representative may tell you that he or she needs to talk with his or her client before making a decision to proceed to the next level. On the other hand, he or she may tell you to go ahead and schedule the district-level conference. It is important to follow any contractual time line for your school district. If the teacher's representative states that the teacher plans to retire or resign, you will need to work with the personnel department to secure a written statement that meets district requirements and ensure that the time line does not lapse before the retirement or resignation is formally submitted (Lawrence & Vachon, 1995, pp 82–85).

Calendar With Suggested Time Line of Actions

The following sample calendar provides a visual representation of the steps in the dismissal process outlined in this guide and correlates with the sample unsatisfactory evaluation documentation for Mr. William Anthony shown in Resource E. The notations that appear in some of the date cells identify the letter or form in Resource E.

The actual time line that you follow and the letters and forms that you use must be consistent with your district's policies and procedures. In addition, the evaluation documentation that you collect and present must be individualized and accurately represent the unsatisfactory teachers' performance.

AUGUST					
	Day				
Week	Monday	Tuesday	Wednesday	Thursday	Friday
1					
2					
3	Send a welcome letter to all staff members assigned to the building with the agenda for Staff Orientation Day (I-A, I-B).	Assign a mentor to each new teacher and identify the mentor teacher in the new teacher's welcome letter (I-C).			Provide orientation for mentor teachers assigned to assist new teachers.
4	Provide orientation for all new teachers.	Provide orientation for all staff members, highlighting philosophy, goals, expectations, and procedures (teacher/school handbook).		Review contractual language, district policies, state statutes, and federal law regarding teacher evaluation and dismissal.	
5					

SEPTEMBER					
	Day				
Week	Monday	Tuesday	Wednesday	Thursday	Friday
1			Provide a written explanation of the evaluation process with samples of evaluation instruments that will be used to evaluate the teaching staff (III-A, III-B, III-C).		
2		Begin informal observations and continue conducting observations throughout the month (III-B). Maintain the summary of informal classroom observations (IV-A1).	Prepare individual teacher files for parental complaints, samples of assignments given to students, notes and student referrals from the teacher regarding discipline problems, letters from the teacher to parents, pending suspensions, and other data (VII).	During classroom visits, collect samples of assignments that teachers give to students, and keep them in individual teacher files (IX).	
3	Provide teaching tips in the weekly staff bulletin. Discuss classroom management and other effective teaching strategies at a staff meeting.	Inform the teacher about parental complaints as they occur, and maintain them in a file (VIII-A, VIII-B).	If the quality of work samples or if classroom management are poor (or both), write a memorandum of concerns to the teacher and offer suggestions for improvement (V).	Prepare individualized letters to teachers identifying the principal as the evaluator and a roster for teachers to initial showing receipt of the letter (II-A, II-B).	Hand deliver the evaluator identification letter to each teacher and have teachers initial receipt of their letters (II-A, II-B).
4	Provide teaching tips in the weekly staff bulletin.	Conduct informal classroom observations (III-B, IV-A1).		Refer the teacher to appropriate sections in the teacher/school handbook (IV-E).	
5	Provide teaching tips in the weekly staff bulletin.	Hold grade-level, subject area, and committee meetings for all teachers throughout the month.			

OCTOBER				
	Day			
Week	Monday	Tuesday	Wednesday	Thursday	Friday
1					Conduct formal observations, provide feedback listing areas of weakness and suggestions for improvement, and give a reasonable length of time for improvement (III-C, IV-A2).
2	Continue conducting daily classroom observations of all teachers (III-B, III-C, IV-A2).	Conduct formal observations, provide feedback listing areas of weaknesses and suggestions for improvement, and give a reasonable length of time for improvement (III-C, IV-A2).	Following the observation, write a memorandum of concerns listing suggestions for improvement and hold a meeting to discuss the concerns (V, V1).	Provide an opportunity for the teacher to observe another teacher in the same school (VI-A). Provide the teacher information on WWW sites about effective teaching (VI-J1).	Continue collecting items for individual teacher files, including parental complaints, discipline referrals, and work samples (VII, VIII-A, VIII-B, IX).
3	Provide teaching tips in the weekly staff bulletin.	Provide an opportunity for the teacher to shadow a successful teacher in another school for the entire day (VI-C). Provide the teacher with information about ordering professional books and resources (VI-K).	Conduct formal observations, provide feedback listing areas of weakness and suggestions for improvement, and give a reasonable length of time for improvement (III-C, IV-A2).	Provide the teacher with a videotape showing successful classroom management strategies and instructional techniques (VI-11).	Provide an opportunity for a teacher from another school to work for a day in the teacher's classroom (VI-D).
4	Provide teaching tips in the weekly staff bulletin. Refer the teacher to the weekly bulletin (VI-L).	Request clarification about the teacher's classroom procedures (VI-M).	Provide opportunities for the teacher to attend workshops conducted by the school district (VI-G1).	Conduct formal observations, provide feedback listing areas of weakness, suggestions for improvement, and give a reasonable length of time for improvement (III-C, IV-A2).	Offer the teacher articles with suggestions for improvement (VI-F1).
5	Provide teaching tips in the weekly staff bulletin.	Prepare an unsatisfactory evaluation binder with a cover page, table of contents, and a divider for each section (A, B).	If the teacher does not improve, issue a letter summarizing the postobservation conference (IV-C). Send a potential unsatisfactory evaluation update letter to your supervisor (X-A1).	If the teacher is improving, note the fact on the observation/evaluation form but reemphasize the suggestions for improvement (III-B, III-C).	Check pertinent historical information about the teacher's background in the school district (Resource F, Suppl-A).

NOVEMBER				
	Day			
Week	Monday	Tuesday	Wednesday	Thursday	Friday
1	Conduct formal observations, provide feedback listing areas of weakness and suggestions for improvement, and give a reasonable length of time for improvement (III-C, IV-A3).	Examine the teacher convention booklet to identify workshops to recommend for the teacher to attend (VI-H).			
2	Provide teaching tips in the weekly staff bulletin.	Continue conducting daily classroom observations of all teachers (IIB, IIIC, IV-A3). Continue collecting items for individual teacher files.	Provide the teacher with videotapes showing successful classroom management strategies and instructional techniques (VI-I2).	Conduct formal observations, provide feedback listing areas of weakness and suggestions for improvement, and give a reasonable length of time for improvement (III-C, IV-A3).	Send a letter to the teacher reviewing assistance provided (VI-N).
3	Provide teaching tips in the weekly staff bulletin.	Offer the teacher articles with suggestions for improvement (VI-F2).	Videotape/audiotape the teacher's class and then meet to discuss specific observations.		Conduct formal observations, provide feedback listing areas of weakness and suggestions for improvement, and give a reasonable length of time for improvement (III-C, IV-A3).
4	Provide teaching tips in the weekly staff bulletin.	Issue a letter summarizing the postobservation conference (IV-C2). Send a potential unsatisfactory evaluation update letter to your supervisor (X-A2).	Maintain contact with the district's personnel department representative and attorney.		

DECEMBER					
	Day				
Week	Monday	Tuesday	Wednesday	Thursday	Friday
1			Conduct formal observations, provide feedback listing areas of weakness and suggestions for improvement, and give a reasonable length of time for improvement (III-C, IV-A4).		Continue conducting daily classroom observations of all teachers (III-B, III-C, IV-A4). Provide an opportunity for the teacher to visit a classroom in the same school (VI-A2, VI-B).
2	Provide teaching tips in the weekly staff bulletin.	Provide the teacher articles on needed areas of improvement (VI-F3).	Provide the teacher with videotapes showing successful classroom management strategies and instructional techniques (VI-I3).	Conduct formal observations, provide feedback listing areas of weakness and suggestions for improvement, and give a reasonable length of time for improvement. III-C, IV-A4).	Continue collecting items for individual teacher files.
3	Conduct formal observations, provide feedback listing areas of weakness and suggestions for improvement, and give a reasonable length of time for improvement (III-C, IV-A4).	Issue a letter summarizing the postobservation conference (IV-C3). Send a potential unsatisfactory evaluation update letter to your supervisor (IX-A3).	Provide opportunities for the teacher to attend workshops conducted by the school district (VI-G2).	Maintain contact with the district's personnel department representative and attorney.	Issue the letter stating the possibility of issuing an unsatisfactory evaluation if the teacher fails to achieve a satisfactory level of performance (X-B).
4	Provide teaching tips in the weekly staff bulletin.				

JANUARY				
Week	Day			
	Monday	Tuesday	Wednesday	Thursday	Friday
1					
2	Provide teaching tips in the weekly staff bulletin. Continue conducting formal and informal classroom observations (III-B, III-C, IV-A5).	Maintain contact with the district's personnel department representative and attorney.	Meet with your supervisor to discuss the unsatisfactory evaluation documentation and draft the unsatisfactory evaluation using the district's established form (X-E).	Prepare the opening and closing statements for the unsatisfactory evaluation conference proceedings (C, D).	Review the unsatisfactory evaluation binder to ensure that all appropriate documentation is included.
3	Provide teaching tips in the weekly staff bulletin and review the schoolwide discipline plan.	Prepare copies of the unsatisfactory evaluation binder (one for the teacher, one for the teacher's representative, one for the school district representative, and one for the principal).			Issue the letter stating the intent to issue an unsatisfactory evaluation in the afternoon and send a copy to the teacher's bargaining unit (X-C).
4	Provide teaching tips in the weekly staff bulletin. Issue the unsatisfactory evaluation.	Send a letter to remind the teacher about the date, time, and location of the unsatisfactory evaluation conference (X-D).	Prepare for the conference and cross-examination. Be knowledgeable of questions that might be asked by the teacher's legal adviser.	Conduct the unsatisfactory evaluation meeting.	
5	Provide teaching tips in the weekly staff bulletin.		Send the unsatisfactory evaluation form to the district's personnel department (X-E).		

FEBRUARY					
	Day				
Week	Monday	Tuesday	Wednesday	Thursday	Friday
1		Continue conducting formal and informal classroom observations (III-B, III-C, IV-A6).	Prepare for presenting the unsatisfactory documentation at the next level(s).		
2	Provide teaching tips in the weekly staff bulletin.	Continue conducting formal and informal classroom observations (III-B, III-C, IV-A6).			
3	Provide teaching tips in the weekly staff bulletin.	Continue conducting formal and informal classroom observations (III-B, III-C, IV-A6).		Maintain contact with the district's personnel department representative and attorney.	
4	Provide teaching tips in the weekly staff bulletin.	Continue conducting formal and informal classroom observations (III-B, III-C, IV-A6).			
5	Provide teaching tips in the weekly staff bulletin.				

	MARCH				
	Day				
Week	Monday	Tuesday	Wednesday	Thursday	Friday
1		Continue conducting formal and informal classroom observations (III-B, III-C, IV-A7).		Maintain contact with the district's personnel department representative and attorney.	
2	Provide teaching tips in the weekly staff bulletin.	Continue conducting formal and informal classroom observations (III-B, III-C, IV-A7).	Begin preparing evaluations for all other staff members.		
3	Provide teaching tips in the weekly staff bulletin.	Continue conducting formal and informal classroom observations (III-B, III-C, IV-A7).		Maintain contact with the district's personnel department representative and attorney.	
4	Provide teaching tips in the weekly staff bulletin.	Continue conducting formal and informal classroom observations (III-B, III-C, IV-A7).			
5	Provide teaching tips in the weekly staff bullctin.	Continue conducting formal and informal classroom observations (III-B, III-C, IV-A7).			

	APRIL				
	Day				
Week	Monday	Tuesday	Wednesday	Thursday	Friday
1					
2	Provide teaching tips in the weekly staff bulletin.	Continue conducting formal and informal classroom observations.			
3	Provide teaching tips in the weekly staff bulletin.	Begin preparing for closing the school year.	Continue conducting formal and informal classroom observations.		
4	Provide teaching tips in the weekly staff bulletin.	Finalize teacher evaluation documentation.	Continue conducting formal and informal classroom observations.		
5	Provide teaching tips to minimize classroom discipline problems during the spring.	Continue conducting formal and informal classroom observations.			

		MAY			
	Day				
Week	Monday	Tuesday	Wednesday	Thursday	Friday
1	Provide teaching tips in the weekly staff bulletin.	Continue conducting formal and informal classroom observations.			
2	Meet individually with teachers requesting further clarification of their strengths and recommendations for improvement.	Continue conducting formal and informal classroom observations.			
3	Complete teacher evaluation conferences.	Continue conducting formal and informal classroom observations.	Summarize the strengths and areas of need of the teaching staff to identify potential mentor teachers and determine staff development needs (Resource F, Suppl-B).	Review the evaluation process and modify procedures and materials as needed for the next school year.	
4	Issue the closing school bulletin.	Continue conducting formal and informal classroom observations.	Send letters to the mentor teachers thanking them for providing support to new teachers.		
5		Continue conducting formal and informal classroom observations. Highlight key points made in the closing bulletin.			

JUNE					
	Day				
Week	Monday	Tuesday	Wednesday	Thursday	Friday
1			Continue conducting formal and informal classroom observations.		
2	Continue conducting formal and informal classroom observations.				
3					
4					
5					

Sample Unsatisfactory Teacher Evaluation Documentation

The following sample unsatisfactory teacher evaluation documentation is provided to show the proposed organizational structure of the binder that you prepare to present the various forms and letters to substantiate the recommendation for dismissal. You may choose to modify the sequence of the sections or even some items within a section depending on your personal preference. Remember, however, that the documentation must be organized in such a way that it is easy for you to present and for the hearing officer to follow. You should use tabs to separate each major section.

A sample opening statement and a sample closing statement are also provided for your reference. These statements are your personal notes and should not be given to the teacher or the teacher's representative.

Any similarity to actual persons living or dead is purely coincidental.

SAMPLE

UNSATISFACTORY TEACHER EVALUATION DOCUMENTATION

for

MR. WILLIAM ANTHONY

SUBMITTED BY

DR. LEMMIE WADE, PRINCIPAL OF

KENNEDY ELEMENTARY SCHOOL

JANUARY _____, 20XX

A

CONTENTS

I. Letters to Staff Members at the Beginning of School
   A. Welcome Staff the School
   B. Orientation Day Agenda
   C. Identification of a Mentor Teacher

II. Identification of Evaluator
   A. Letter Identifying the Teacher's Evaluator
   B. School Roster for Teachers' Initials Acknowledging Receipt of Evaluation Letter

III. Observation/Evaluation Procedures for the School
   A. Letter Explaining the Evaluation Process
   B. Informal Observation/Evaluation Form
   C. Formal Observation/Evaluation Form

IV. Observation Documentation
   A. Summaries of Monthly Observations of Staff Members
   B. Observations of the Teacher
   C. Summary Letters of Conferences Following Observations of the Teacher

V. Memoranda of Concerns

VI. Letters/Documents Relative to Assistance Provided
   A. Visiting a Classroom in the Same School
   B. Peer Observation Form
   C. Shadowing by the Teacher in Another School
   D. Visitation by a Teacher From Another School
   E. Section in the Teachers' Handbook
   F. Articles to Read
   G. Workshop to Attend
   H. Convention to Attend
   I. Videotapes to View
   J. World Wide Web (WWW) Internet Sites
   K. Ordering from a Publisher's Catalog
   L. Weekly Bulletins
   M. Classroom Procedures
   N. Review of Assistance

VII. Discipline Referrals

VIII. Parental Complaints
   A. Letters Informing the Teacher About Parental Complaints
   B. Parental Complaints Filed Against the Teacher (Letters, Telephone Calls)

IX. Work Samples

X. Unsatisfactory Evaluation Letters and Evaluation
   A. Memoranda to the Principal's Supervisor Summarizing Observations, Conferences, and Support Provided to the Teacher
   B. Failure to Achieve a Satisfactory Level of Performance
   C. Intent to Issue an Unsatisfactory Evaluation
   D. Meeting Reminder
   E. Unsatisfactory Evaluation

OPENING STATEMENT FOR THE UNSATISFACTORY EVALUATION CONFERENCE FOR MR. WILLIAM ANTHONY

An unsatisfactory evaluation is issued when a teacher fails to respond to the efforts that were made to help improve his or her teaching performance and subsequent failure to develop a behavioral management plan to reduce negative student behaviors. When this occurs, teaching performance is poor, and student misbehavior has a negative impact on student learning.

Prior to issuance of this unsatisfactory evaluation, contractual procedures were followed to ensure that procedural and substantive due process were applied. Part III, Section 2, on Page 16 of the contract identifies the steps that are required by ABC School District to evaluate unsatisfactory teachers.

William Anthony has been a teacher in the ABC School District since 20XX, working at King Elementary and Springdale Elementary Schools. He was evaluated by Mrs. Adele Simon during the 20XX-20XX school year and by Mr. Victor Harris during the 20XX-20XX and 20XX-20XX school years. Both supervisors found his teaching skills to be below average. During those two separate assignments in different schools, Mr. Anthony was unable to attain and maintain a level of acceptable teaching performance.

Mr. Anthony is licensed in elementary education and holds certification to work in the capacity of a teacher at grade levels 3 through 6 in all subject areas.

The following letters are in Mr. William Anthony's employee file in the Personnel Department regarding his unsatisfactory teaching performance:

Date	Principal	Summary of Statements Regarding Performance
20XX-20XX	Ms. Adele Simon	To be completed
20XX-20XX	Mr. Victor Harris	To be completed

The following unsatisfactory evaluations are in Mr. William Anthony's employee file in the Personnel Department warning him about unsatisfactory teaching performance:

Date	Principal	Summary of Statements Regarding Performance
20XX-20XX	Mr. Victor Harris	To be completed

A summary follows of Mr. William Anthony's absenteeism during the past 3 years:

Year	Number Days Absent	Total Hours Absent
20XX-20XX	25	195.5
20XX-20XX	12	93.0
20XX-20XX	10	139.0

C

On two different occasions, Mr. Anthony filed for workers' compensation related to teaching performance.

Year	Claim	Disposition
20XX-20XX	Back injury caused by an attempt to break up a student fight	Not approved
20XX-20XX	Stress caused by numerous observations by the principal	Not approved

During his assignment at Kennedy Elementary School, he has been

- Absent 10 times for a total of 79 hours:

Dates	Number of Hours	Reason
9/9/XX	8	Illness
9/23/XX	8	Court appearance
9/24/XX	8	Illness
10/9/XX	8	Illness
10/12/XX	8	Illness
10/30/XX	7	Illness
11/16/XX	8	Family emergency
12/10/XX	8	Illness
12/11/XX	8	Illness
1/8/XX	8	Illness

- Late to work 9 times for a total of 5.7 hours:

Dates	Number of Hours	Reason
9/4/XX	.5	Car trouble
9/22/XX	.5	Overslept
10/15/XX	.5	Overslept
10/19/XX	.5	Traffic on expressway
11/2/XX	1.5	Personal errand
11/3/XX	.1	Flat tire
11/23/XX	.1	Overslept
12/7/XX	1.5	Car trouble
1/13/XX	.5	Could not find car keys

- Charged with the following actions of misconduct related to teaching performance:

Date	Charge	Disposition
10/5/XX	Leaving students unsupervised	Verbal warning
10/20/XX	Use of undue force on a student	Written reprimand
11/4/XX	Failure to report to playground duty	Letter in the central administration file
12/3/XX	Use of undue physical force to detain a student	Three-day suspension without pay

Parents have called the principal and have written letters about the conditions in Mr. Anthony's classroom.

Just-Cause Requirements

- The teacher evaluation process for the school district and school was made known to all teachers in the school, and the process was consistently followed.

- Mr. Anthony was not singled out and the same standards were applied to all teachers.

- Observations of Mr. Anthony included all phases of his assignments.

- A continuous and accurately dated file of all observations and evaluations was maintained.

- Mr. Anthony received written memoranda of concerns that specified the exact nature of his teaching deficiencies.

- In each memorandum of concerns, Mr. Anthony received specific suggestions for correcting his teaching deficiencies and suggestions relative how to achieve a satisfactory level of teaching performance.

- Mr. Anthony was given a reasonable period of time for necessary improvements.

- Mr. Anthony was informed that failure to achieve an acceptable level of performance by January 14, 20XX, would result in the issuance of an unsatisfactory evaluation.

Despite the opportunities to improve his teaching, Mr. Anthony has not achieved the acceptable level of teaching performance.

In closing, Mr. William Anthony's overall teaching performance is related to undesirable student behaviors. Moreover, he failed to respond to the efforts that were made to help improve his teaching performance, and he failed to develop effective teaching strategies, including a classroom management plan to reduce negative student behavior. These are justifications for issuing an unsatisfactory teacher evaluation.

At this point, I will provide you with copies of the documentation to support the unsatisfactory evaluation that has been issued to Mr. Anthony.

(NOTE: This opening statement should not be included in the Unsatisfactory Teacher Evaluation Document. It should be read at the beginning of each hearing.)

ABC SCHOOL DISTRICT   **KENNEDY ELEMENTARY SCHOOL**

1584 South Pineview Drive
Crescent Ridge, California 70799
(916) 444-4444

August 16, 20XX

Dear Staff:

I hope you are having a restful and pleasant summer vacation. The 20XX-20XX school year will present new challenges to all of us—new students, new teacher, and new textbooks and instructional materials.

This school year will provide an opportunity for us to provide an excellent education for all of our students. As always, we will continue to work together to make our school the best in the ABC School District.

I am very enthusiastic about working with you this school year to meet the greater challenges ahead in educating our children—our most precious resource. In preparation for our first meeting of the school year, I am enclosing a copy of the organization day agenda.

Again, welcome back! This will be the best year ever at Kennedy Elementary School.

Sincerely,

Lemmie Wade, PhD
Principal

Enclosure

ABC SCHOOL DISTRICT   **KENNEDY ELEMENTARY SCHOOL**

1584 South Pineview Drive
Crescent Ridge, California 70799
(916) 444-4444

ORGANIZATION DAY AGENDA
AUGUST 24, 20XX

8:00-8:30 A.M.   Continental Breakfast/Social in Cafeteria

8:30-8:50 A.M.   Welcome
        Good news celebration!
        New teacher introductions
        New support staff introductions

8:50-11:50 A.M.   Staff Orientation
        Review opening day procedures
        New teacher handbook
        Attendance procedures
        Playground duty schedules
        Lunch duty schedule
        Specialist schedule
        Librarian schedule
        Specialists (e.g., counselor, psychologist)
        School climate
        School district discipline plan
        Kennedy School discipline plan
        Classroom discipline plans due September 2, 20XX
        Safe and orderly classrooms
        Entrance and dismissal procedures
        Lunchroom procedures
        Fire drill and emergency procedures
        Staff evaluations
        Evaluation procedures
        Preobservation conferences
        Postobservation conferences
        Other discussion items
        First day meeting—August 27, 20XX at 8:00 A.M.
        Open house—September 23, 20XX at 7:00 P.M.
        Parent/teacher conferences—November 3, 20XX

12:00 noon-1:00 P.M.   Catered Lunch in School Cafeteria

1:05-3:00 P.M.   Classroom Preparation

3:00-3:30 P.M.   All Staff Meeting in Cafeteria
        Announcements and final opening day information

I-B

ABC SCHOOL DISTRICT   **KENNEDY ELEMENTARY SCHOOL**

1584 South Pineview Drive
Crescent Ridge, California 70799
(916) 444-4444

August 17, 20XX

Mr. William Anthony
4815 West Second Street
Crescent Ridge, California 70798

Dear Mr. Anthony:

Welcome to Kennedy Elementary School. I want to make this an educationally rewarding and successful school year for you. This will be the best year ever for staff and students at Kennedy Elementary School.

To help you adjust to your new school, I have assigned Mr. Scott Larson in Room 106 to serve as your mentor teacher to answer questions you may have about the school and to assist you throughout the school year. I am also here to assist you in any way possible to make this a successful school year. Please feel free to contact me to discuss any concerns you may have about Kennedy Elementary School.

Again, welcome to Kennedy Elementary School. I am happy to have you join our staff, and I look forward to observing the exciting learning activities in your classroom.

Sincerely,

Lemmie Wade, PhD
Principal

ABC school district   **KENNEDY ELEMENTARY SCHOOL**

1584 South Pineview Drive
Crescent Ridge, California 70799
(916) 444-4444

September 17, 20XX

Mr. William Anthony
4815 West Second Street
Crescent Ridge, California 70798

Dear Mr. Anthony:

The primary purpose of performance evaluation is to improve teaching performance and promote professional growth. This is consistent with the contract
between the ABC Board of School Directors and the ABC Teachers Education
Association. The evaluation procedures for this school year will ensure that a
cooperative plan is established by the teacher and the evaluator.

Teacher evaluations are a necessary part of educational administration. They
should be viewed by teachers as a learning experience, as a way for both the
teacher and the administrator to grow in understanding and knowledge.

Teacher strengths will be discussed so that they can enhance the learning environment and to further professional development. Teacher weaknesses will be
identified so that appropriate methods can be devised to reduce or alleviate those
weaknesses.

Part III, Section A of the master teachers' contract states that the evaluator must
be made known to the teacher by name and title. Accordingly, you are informed
that your performance evaluation during the 20XX-20XX school year shall be
conducted by me with possible collaboration with other administrative and
supervisory staff assigned to Kennedy Elementary School. In the event that someone else must serve in my capacity, that person will conduct your evaluation.

If you have any questions or concerns regarding this matter, please contact me.

Sincerely,

Lemmie Wade, PhD
Principal

II-A

KENNEDY ELEMENTARY SCHOOL
STAFF ROSTER
SEPTEMBER 17, 20XX

INITIAL	NAME
————	Adams, Hilda
————	Anthony, William
————	Barnett, Michelle
————	Craine, Diane
————	Dailey, Dawna
————	Elliott, Lucia
————	Haggerty, Faye
————	Hall, Rachel
————	Hernandez, Rosa
————	Huebner, Shelly
————	Larson, Scott
————	Maas-Carns, Camille
————	Margis, Cindy
————	McNeal, Donald
————	Najam, Sara
————	O'Donnell, Marlene
————	Patterson, Gary
————	Thomas, Stewart
————	Williams, Darren
————	Zwicke, Gail

ABC SCHOOL DISTRICT   **KENNEDY ELEMENTARY SCHOOL**

1584 South Pineview Drive
Crescent Ridge, California 70799
(916) 444-4444

September 1, 20XX

Dear Staff:

This year, three different approaches will be used to evaluate teachers: informal, formal, and year-end teacher observations/evaluations. Descriptions of these procedures follow:

1. Informal Observations/Evaluations (Formative)

Informal observations/evaluations will consist of short classroom observations/evaluations. An observation checklist will be used to give teachers immediate feedback on their performance. Teachers should expect more than three informal observations.

2. Formal Observations/Evaluations (Formative)

Formal observations/evaluations will be conducted for teachers scheduled for a district-mandated evaluation. A formal observation/evaluation may be used for unscheduled teacher evaluations.

A formal evaluation will last for the duration of the class period; however, it may be shorter. Teachers scheduled for formal evaluations are to schedule two preobservation conferences and two postobservation conferences.

During the preobservation conference, teachers are to explain their lesson plans and the methodology they plan to use in the lesson. The planning conference should take about 15 minutes. At the preobservation conference, teachers will receive an observation/evaluation form. Before the postobservation conference, teachers are to complete this form by checking the column that they believe best describes their teaching.

Within five days after the formal observation/evaluation, a postobservation conference should be held. During this conference, the teacher's strengths and weaknesses, and suggestions for improvement, if necessary, will be discussed.

3. Year-End Evaluation (Summative)

This is the final observation/evaluation conference of the school year. This conference will be held during April or May. A written statement will be placed on the official district evaluation form.

Enclosed are copies of evaluation instruments that will be used to evaluate your teaching performance this school year. If you have any questions, please see my secretary to schedule a meeting with me.

Sincerely,

Lemmie Wade, PhD
Principal

Enclosures

KENNEDY ELEMENTARY SCHOOL
INFORMAL OBSERVATION/EVALUATION FORM

Date _____ Time of day _____ Class period _____
Teacher _____ Subject/Grade _____
Total students assigned to class/In class ____ / ____ Evaluation number _____

Scale: 1 = *Outstanding*   3 = *Average*   5 = *Unsatisfactory*
                2 = *Above average*   4 = *Fair*   NA = *Not Applicable*

(NOTE: Insert criteria established by the school district.)

Criteria	1	2	3	4	5	NA
1. Has lesson plans that clearly state objectives and instructional strategies						
2. Provides evidence of effective instruction						
3. Uses appropriate and varied instructional materials/techniques						
4. Organizes and plans lessons						
5. Motivates students						
6. Uses appropriate discipline techniques to maintain classroom control						
7. Clearly communicates the lesson to students						
8. Uses class time efficiently						
9. Maintains an organized and attractive classroom						
10. Appropriately arranges furniture for instruction (e.g., large group, small group)						
11. Maintains neat, attractive, and educationally relevant bulletin boards						
12. Demonstrates knowledge of the curriculum						

Comments _____
_____

If you wish to discuss this observation/evaluation checklist with me, please see my secretary to schedule an appointment with me.

Principal _____

III-B

KENNEDY ELEMENTARY SCHOOL
FORMAL OBSERVATION/EVALUATION FORM

Date _____   Time of day _____   Class period _____
Teacher _____   Subject/Grade _____
Total students assigned to class/In class _____   Evaluation number _____

Scale: 1 = *Outstanding*   3 = *Average*   5 = *Unsatisfactory*
         2 = *Above average*   4 = *Fair*   NA = *Not Applicable*

(NOTE: Insert specific criteria under the general categories, based on district standards.)

A. PLANNING/INSTRUCTIONAL STRATEGIES USED	1	2	3	4	5	NA
1.						
2.						
3.						
4.						
4.						
5.						
6.						
7.						
8.						
9.						
10.						
11.						
12.						
13.						
14.						
15.						
16.						

Comments _____
_____
_____

B. UNDERSTANDING THE CURRICULUM	1	2	3	4	5	NA
1.						
2.						
3.						

Comments _____
_____
_____

III-C

C. ASSESSMENT OF INSTRUCTIONAL PLAN	1	2	3	4	5	NA
1.						
2.						
3.						
4.						
4.						
5.						
6.						
7.						
8.						
9.						
10.						
11.						
12.						
13.						
14.						
15.						

Comments _____

_____

_____

D. CLASSROOM MANAGEMENT	1	2	3	4	5	NA
1.						
2.						
3.						
4.						
5.						

Comments _____

_____

_____

E. CLASSROOM ENVIRONMENT	1	2	3	4	5	NA
1.						
2.						
3.						
4.						
5.						

Comments _____

_____

_____

F. SCHOOLWIDE INVOLVEMENT	1	2	3	4	5	NA
List your involvement in school activities:						

1. _____
2. _____
3. _____

Comments _____
_____
_____

G. PROFESSIONAL DEVELOPMENT	1	2	3	4	5	NA
List your involvement in professional development activities:						

1. _____
2. _____
3. _____

Comments _____
_____
_____

If you wish to discuss this observation/evaluation checklist with me, please see my secretary to schedule an appointment with me.

Principal _____

ABC SCHOOL DISTRICT

KENNEDY ELEMENTARY SCHOOL

1584 South Pineview Drive
Crescent Ridge, California 70799
(916) 444-4444

SUMMARIES OF MONTHLY OBSERVATIONS OF STAFF MEMBERS

Attached are completed observation forms that show observations conducted of staff members during the 20XX-20XX school year.

SUMMARY OF INFORMAL CLASSROOM OBSERVATIONS
SEPTEMBER 20XX

SCHOOL: <u>Kennedy Elementary</u>   PRINCIPAL: <u>Lemmie Wade</u>

(Insert the dates that school is in session along the top row and the names of all teaching staff members in the first column. Place a check mark in the grid to indicate that an observation was made. Circle the check mark for a formal observation.)

Staff Member	1	2	3	6	7	8	9	10	13	14	15	16	17	20	21	22	23	24	27	28
Adams, H.																				
Anthony, W.																				
Barnett, M.																				
Craine, D.																				
Dailey, D.																				
Elliott, L.																				
Haggerty, F.																				
Hall, R.																				
Hernandez, R.																				
Huebner, S.																				
Larson, S.																				
Maas-Carns, C.																				
Margis, C.																				
McNeal, D.																				
Najam, S.																				
O'Donnell, M.																				
Patterson, G.																				
Thomas, S.																				
Williams, D.																				
Zwicke, G.																				

SUMMARY OF INFORMAL CLASSROOM OBSERVATIONS
OCTOBER 20XX

SCHOOL: <u>Kennedy Elementary</u>   PRINCIPAL: <u>Lemmie Wade</u>

(Insert the dates that school is in session along the top row and the names of all teaching staff members in the first column. Place a check mark in the grid to indicate that an observation was made. Circle the check mark for a formal observation.)

Staff Member	1	2	3	6	7	8	9	10	13	14	15	16	17	20	21	22	23	24	27	28	29	30
Adams, H.																						
Anthony, W.																						
Barnett, M.																						
Craine, D.																						
Dailey, D.																						
Elliott, L.																						
Haggerty, F.																						
Hall, R.																						
Hernandez, R.																						
Huebner, S.																						
Larson, S.																						
Maas-Carns, C.																						
Margis, C.																						
McNeal, D.																						
Najam, S.																						
O'Donnell, M.																						
Patterson, G.																						
Thomas, S.																						
Williams, D.																						
Zwicke, G.																						

SUMMARY OF INFORMAL CLASSROOM OBSERVATIONS
NOVEMBER 20XX

SCHOOL: <u>Kennedy Elementary</u>   PRINCIPAL: <u>Lemmie Wade</u>

(Insert the dates that school is in session along the top row and the names of all teaching staff members in the first column. Place a check mark in the grid to indicate that an observation was made. Circle the check mark for a formal observation.)

Staff Member	1	2	3	6	7	8	9	10	13	14	15	16	17	20	21	22	23	24	27	28	29	30
Adams, H.																						
Anthony, W.																						
Barnett, M.																						
Craine, D.																						
Dailey, D.																						
Elliott, L.																						
Haggerty, F.																						
Hall, R.																						
Hernandez, R.																						
Huebner, S.																						
Larson, S.																						
Maas-Carns, C.																						
Margis, C.																						
McNeal, D.																						
Najam, S.																						
O'Donnell, M.																						
Patterson, G.																						
Thomas, S.																						
Williams, D.																						
Zwicke, G.																						

SUMMARY OF INFORMAL CLASSROOM OBSERVATIONS
DECEMBER 20XX

SCHOOL: <u>Kennedy Elementary</u>   PRINCIPAL: <u>Lemmie Wade</u>

(Insert the dates that school is in session along the top row and the names of all teaching staff members in the first column. Place a check mark in the grid to indicate that an observation was made. Circle the check mark for a formal observation.)

Staff Member	1	2	3	6	7	8	9	10	13	14	15	16	17	20	21	22	23	24	27	28	29	30
Adams, H.																						
Anthony, W.																						
Barnett, M.																						
Craine, D.																						
Dailey, D.																						
Elliott, L.																						
Haggerty, F.																						
Hall, R.																						
Hernandez, R.																						
Huebner, S.																						
Larson, S.																						
Maas-Carns, C.																						
Margis, C.																						
McNeal, D.																						
Najam, S.																						
O'Donnell, M.																						
Patterson, G.																						
Thomas, S.																						
Williams, D.																						
Zwicke, G.																						

SUMMARY OF INFORMAL CLASSROOM OBSERVATIONS
JANUARY 20XX

SCHOOL: <u>Kennedy Elementary</u>   PRINCIPAL: <u>Lemmie Wade</u>

(Insert the dates that school is in session along the top row and the names of all teaching staff members in the first column. Place a check mark in the grid to indicate that an observation was made. Circle the check mark for a formal observation.)

Staff Member	1	2	3	6	7	8	9	10	13	14	15	16	17	20	21	22	23	24	27	28	29	30
Adams, H.																						
Anthony, W.																						
Barnett, M.																						
Craine, D.																						
Dailey, D.																						
Elliott, L.																						
Haggerty, F.																						
Hall, R.																						
Hernandez, R.																						
Huebner, S.																						
Larson, S.																						
Maas-Carns, C.																						
Margis, C.																						
McNeal, D.																						
Najam, S.																						
O'Donnell, M.																						
Patterson, G.																						
Thomas, S.																						
Williams, D.																						
Zwicke, G.																						

SUMMARY OF INFORMAL CLASSROOM OBSERVATIONS
FEBRUARY 20XX

SCHOOL: <u>Kennedy Elementary</u>   PRINCIPAL: <u>Lemmie Wade</u>

(Insert the dates that school is in session along the top row and the names of all teaching staff members in the first column. Place a check mark in the grid to indicate that an observation was made. Circle the check mark for a formal observation.)

Staff Member	1	2	3	6	7	8	9	10	13	14	15	16	17	20	21	22	23	24	27	28	29	30
Adams, H.																						
Anthony, W.																						
Barnett, M.																						
Craine, D.																						
Dailey, D.																						
Elliott, L.																						
Haggerty, F.																						
Hall, R.																						
Hernandez, R.																						
Huebner, S.																						
Larson, S.																						
Maas-Carns, C.																						
Margis, C.																						
McNeal, D.																						
Najam, S.																						
O'Donnell, M.																						
Patterson, G.																						
Thomas, S.																						
Williams, D.																						
Zwicke, G.																						

SUMMARY OF INFORMAL CLASSROOM OBSERVATIONS
MARCH 20XX

SCHOOL: <u>Kennedy Elementary</u>　　　　PRINCIPAL: <u>Lemmie Wade</u>

(Insert the dates that school is in session along the top row and the names of all teaching staff members in the first column. Place a check mark in the grid to indicate that an observation was made. Circle the check mark for a formal observation.)

Staff Member	1	2	3	6	7	8	9	10	13	14	15	16	17	20	21	22	23	24	27	28	29	30
Adams, H.																						
Anthony, W.																						
Barnett, M.																						
Craine, D.																						
Dailey, D.																						
Elliott, L.																						
Haggerty, F.																						
Hall, R.																						
Hernandez, R.																						
Huebner, S.																						
Larson, S.																						
Maas-Carns, C.																						
Margis, C.																						
McNeal, D.																						
Najam, S.																						
O'Donnell, M.																						
Patterson, G.																						
Thomas, S.																						
Williams, D.																						
Zwicke, G.																						

ABC SCHOOL DISTRICT   **KENNEDY ELEMENTARY SCHOOL**

1584 South Pineview Drive
Crescent Ridge, California 70799
(916) 444-4444

CLASSROOM OBSERVATIONS OF MR. WILLIAM ANTHONY

Attached are completed observation forms used when classroom observations were made of Mr. William Anthony:

Informal Observations   _____
Formal Observations   _____
Total   _____

KENNEDY ELEMENTARY SCHOOL
INFORMAL OBSERVATION/EVALUATION FORM

Date _____ Time of day _____ Class period _____

Teacher _____ Subject/Grade _____

Total students assigned to class/In class ___ / ___ Evaluation number _____

Scale: 1 = *Outstanding*   3 = *Average*   5 = *Unsatisfactory*
          2 = *Above average*   4 = *Fair*   NA = *Not Applicable*

(NOTE: Insert criteria established by the school district.)

Criteria	1	2	3	4	5	NA
1. Has lesson plans that clearly state objectives and instructional strategies						
2. Provides evidence of effective instruction						
3. Uses appropriate and varied instructional materials/techniques						
4. Organizes and plans lessons						
5. Motivates students						
6. Uses appropriate discipline techniques to maintain classroom control						
7. Clearly communicates the lesson to students						
8. Uses class time efficiently						
9. Maintains an organized and attractive classroom						
10. Appropriately arranges furniture for instruction (e.g., large group, small group)						
11. Maintains neat, attractive, and educationally relevant bulletin boards						
12. Demonstrates knowledge of the curriculum						

Comments _____

_____

_____

If you wish to discuss this observation/evaluation form with me, please see my secretary to schedule an appointment.

Principal _____

KENNEDY ELEMENTARY SCHOOL
FORMAL OBSERVATION/EVALUATION FORM

Date _____ Time of day _____ Class period _____

Teacher _____ Subject/Grade _____

Total students assigned to class/In class ___ / ___ Evaluation number _____

Scale: 1 = *Outstanding*   3 = *Average*   5 = *Unsatisfactory*
        2 = *Above average*   4 = *Fair*   NA = *Not Applicable*

(NOTE: Insert specific criteria under the general categories, based on district standards.)

A. PLANNING/INSTRUCTIONAL STRATEGIES USED	1	2	3	4	5	NA
1.						
2.						
3.						
4.						
5.						

Comments _____

_____

_____

B. UNDERSTANDING THE CURRICULUM	1	2	3	4	5	NA
1.						
2.						
3.						
4.						
5.						

Comments _____

_____

_____

C. ASSESSMENT OF INSTRUCTIONAL PLAN	1	2	3	4	5	NA
1.						
2.						
3.						
4.						
5.						

Comments _____

_____

_____

D. CLASSROOM MANAGEMENT	1	2	3	4	5	NA
1.						
2.						
3.						
4.						
5.						

Comments _____

_____

_____

E. CLASSROOM ENVIRONMENT	1	2	3	4	5	NA
1.						
2.						
3.						
4.						
5.						

Comments _____

_____

_____

F. SCHOOLWIDE INVOLVEMENT	1	2	3	4	5	NA
List your involvement in school activities:						

1. _____
2. _____
3. _____

Comments _____
_____
_____

G. PROFESSIONAL DEVELOPMENT	1	2	3	4	5	NA
List your involvement in professional development activities:						

1. _____
2. _____
3. _____

Comments _____
_____
_____

If you wish to discuss this observation/evaluation checklist with me, please see my secretary to schedule an appointment with me.

Principal _____

ABC SCHOOL DISTRICT   **KENNEDY ELEMENTARY SCHOOL**

                                        1584 South Pineview Drive
                                        Crescent Ridge, California 70799
                                        (916) 444-4444

LETTERS SUMMARIZING MEETINGS
FOLLOWING CLASSROOM OBSERVATIONS

Attached are letters issued to Mr. William Anthony summarizing meetings held following classroom observations:

October 27, 20XX
November 23, 20XX
December 14, 20XX

IV-C

ABC SCHOOL DISTRICT   **KENNEDY ELEMENTARY SCHOOL**

1584 South Pineview Drive
Crescent Ridge, California 70799
(916) 444-4444

October 27, 20XX

Mr. William Anthony
Kennedy Elementary School

This letter serves as a summary of our meeting, which was held in my office on Friday, October 22, 20XX, at 3:30 P.M. I began the meeting by stating my concerns about your inability to effectively manage your classroom. My concerns were as follows:

1. Lack of effective classroom management
2. Failure to develop effective lesson plans
3. Failure to maintain class control

We also discussed the support materials and opportunities that were provided for you. In addition, I gave you the following suggestions to improve your classroom management skills:

1. Read the two articles on classroom management.
2. View the videotape on positive classroom management.
3. Attend workshops on classroom management, teaching reading in the intermediate grades, and cooperative learning.
4. Review the teachers' handbook on lesson plans, the homework policy, schoolwide rules and consequences, and student discipline.
5. Group students for small group instruction.
6. Increase mobility to monitor students during practice and do not sit behind your desk.
7. Post classroom rules and consequences.
8. Use the successful classroom management, organizational skills, and instructional techniques observed when you were released to observe successful 5th grade teachers.

I want to continue supporting your efforts to improve your classroom management skills and stand ready to assist you in improving your teaching effectiveness.

Sincerely,

Lemmie Wade, PhD
Principal

ABC SCHOOL DISTRICT   **KENNEDY ELEMENTARY SCHOOL**

1584 South Pineview Drive
Crescent Ridge, California 70799
(916) 444-4444

November 23, 20XX

Mr. William Anthony
Kennedy Elementary School

Dear Mr. Anthony:

This letter serves as a summary of our meeting, which was held in my office on Wednesday, November 10, 20XX, at 3:30 P.M. I began the meeting stating my concerns about your inability to effectively manage your classroom. My concerns were as follows:

1. Lack of effective classroom management
2. Failure to carry out lesson plans
3. Failure to maintain class control
4. The amount of off-task student behavior

We also discussed support materials and opportunities that were provided for you. In addition, I gave you the following recommendations to improve your classroom management skills:

1. View the videotape on increasing student achievement through "cooperative learning" and "creating an atmosphere for positive student interaction."
2. Review the teacher handbook sections on report cards, parent complaints, and communication strategies for parent-teacher conferences.
3. Group students for small group instruction.
4. Do not let students go into the hallway to study.
5. Establish clear procedures for students to get materials and use the pencil sharpener.
6. Increase your mobility to monitor students during practice and do not sit behind your desk.

I stand ready to assist you in improving your teaching effectiveness; however, failure to improve your teaching performance by January 14, 20XX, may result in an unsatisfactory teacher evaluation.

Sincerely,

Lemmie Wade, PhD
Principal

IV-C2

ABC SCHOOL DISTRICT   **KENNEDY ELEMENTARY SCHOOL**

1584 South Pineview Drive
Crescent Ridge, California 70799
(916) 444-4444

December 14, 20XX

Mr. William Anthony
Kennedy Elementary School

Dear Mr. Anthony:

This letter serves as summary of our meeting, which was held in my office on Friday, December 10, 20XX, at 3:30 P.M. I began the meeting stating my concerns about your inability to effectively manage your classroom. My concerns were as follows:

1. Lack of effective classroom management
2. Failure to design and implement effective lesson plans
3. Failure to maintain class control

We also discussed support materials and opportunities that were provided for you. In addition, I gave you the following recommendations to improve your classroom management skills:

1. Read articles "Creating a Positive Classroom Learning Experience," "How to Prepare an Effective Reading Lesson," and "Discipline—A Step-by-Step Guide for Elementary School Teachers."
2. View the videotape on preparing lesson plans.
3. Group students for small group instruction.
4. Increase your mobility to monitor students during individual practice and do not sit behind your desk.
5. Post classroom rules and consequences.
6. Change your current reward system.

I stand ready to assist you in improving your teaching effectiveness; however, failure to improve your teaching performance by January 14, 20XX, will result in an unsatisfactory teacher evaluation with a recommendation for your dismissal from the school district.

Sincerely,

Lemmie Wade, PhD
Principal

ABC SCHOOL DISTRICT

KENNEDY ELEMENTARY SCHOOL

1584 South Pineview Drive
Crescent Ridge, California 70799
(916) 444-4444

MEMORANDA OF CONCERNS

Attached are memoranda of concerns issued to Mr. William Anthony:

October 1, 20XX
November 4, 20XX

ABC SCHOOL DISTRICT   **KENNEDY ELEMENTARY SCHOOL**

1584 South Pineview Drive
Crescent Ridge, California 70799
(916) 444-4444

DATE: October 1, 20XX
TO: Mr. William Anthony
FROM: Dr. Lemmie Wade
RE: Memorandum of Concerns #1

During the past month, numerous informal and formal observations/evaluations were conducted of your classroom teaching. In addition to providing you with a copy of these observations/evaluations, which included a list of suggestions to improve your teaching performance, postobservation conferences were held and a summary of each conference was sent to you. This memorandum focuses on the importance of having a good classroom management plan so that you can teach students effectively and provides examples of concerns as well as suggestions relative to how you can improve. As a follow-up to this memorandum, informal observations will be conducted to assess how well you have implemented those suggestions. Toward the end of the month, you will receive a memorandum of accomplishment that indicates progress that you have made with regard to each of these suggestions.

Concern #1—Classroom Management (Procedures)

Your classroom is an unsafe environment. In my opinion, little or no learning is taking place, and the lack of classroom management procedures has a negative impact on the children. In fact, on Thursday, September 26, 20XX, at approximately 10:10 A.M., I observed students wandering around the room talking to each other while you were standing in front of the class trying to teach. Some students were shouting out answers, and other students were yelling at other classmate to be quiet. You sent three students to the office for talking out of turn. By noon, you had sent 10 students to the office for minor infractions, such as talking out of turn, not having supplies, and chewing gum.

Suggestions

1. Develop a classroom management plan for progressive discipline.
2. Include rewards and incentives as part of your classroom management plan.
3. Post your classroom management plan (e.g., rules, rewards, consequences).
4. Use good work as a reward (e.g., computer time, free time).
5. Develop a flyer, brochure, or letter to inform parents about your classroom management plan.
6. Include your classroom procedures as part of your classroom management plan.

7. Develop some nonverbal strategies to get student attention (e.g., firm look, hand clap, light signal, hand or finger sign).
8. Be consistent with consequences for misbehavior.
9. Try to give children an option to choose their punishment.
10. Make sure the punishment is punishment and is not considered to be a fun activity.
11. Do not send students to the office for minor infractions (e.g., chewing gum, no pencil).
12. Report major problems to the principal.
13. Do not ignore children who are misbehaving.
14. After each break (e.g., winter recess, spring break, track break), remind students about classroom rules.

Concern 2—Classroom Management (Morning Arrival Procedures)

You must be on time to pick up your students on the playground and escort them quietly to their classroom. As you know, a warning bell rings at 8:50 A.M., signaling teachers to pick up their students by 9:00 A.M. Several times, you have been late in picking up your students. For example, on Friday, September 15, 20XX, you were eight minutes late because you were getting material from the supply room. Your students were left unsupervised on the playground, which resulted in a student fight. Moreover, you yelled at the children saying, "Why are you fighting? Stop it, stop it." I intervened, stopping the fight. If you had been on time, your presence may have prevented this fight. You must be proactive to prevent potential problems.

Suggestions

1. Arrive by 8:58 A.M. to greet and pick up your students on the playground.
2. Develop procedures for walking in the corridor (e.g., arrival, recess, lunch, dismissal).
3. Assign a student line monitor to lead the students into the school.
4. Know the names of your students so you can talk with them in the morning on the playground.
5. Try to smile at each student at least once per day.
6. Start the school day by providing a safe and orderly climate in which children can learn.
7. Develop a plan to handle potential early-morning troublemakers.
8. Refrain from bluffing students about what you will do if they misbehave.
9. Explain the reason for punishment for misbehavior, but refrain from saying, "If you don't behave in line, the whole class will stay in for recess."
10. React calmly and quickly to discipline problems.
11. Don't argue with a student or students.

Concern 3—Classroom Management (Beginning Morning Activities)

You must establish morning routines so your class gets off to a good start. I have observed students running into your classroom to sit near their friends in the back of the room. In my opinion, you do not have a floor plan or seating chart for students. Also, there appears to be no plan for getting the school day off to a good start. For example, on Tuesday, September 16, 20XX, you did not take attendance.

Suggestions

1. Develop morning routines to get your class off to a good start.
2. Post a daily schedule and discuss any changes each morning. Include art, music, physical education, and any pullout programs in this schedule.
3. Account for every minute in the school day.
4. Give clear step-by-step directions to students.
5. Develop procedures to pass out textbooks.
6. Arrange seating so you can see the children and, if necessary, move them to different seat locations.
7. Design a floor plan for small group activities.
8. Relocate your bookcases to establish clear traffic patterns.
9. Design learning centers for computers, reading, mathematics, and so forth.
10. Keep learning center tables organized and stocked with necessary materials.
11. Do not allow troublemakers to sit together.
12. Develop a plan for handling playground equipment for recess and lunchtime.
13. Avoid embarrassing students in front of their peers.
14. Refrain from telling a student that he or she will not be allowed to return to your classroom.
15. Do not allow children to wander around the classroom.
16. Do not allow children to throw crayons in the classroom.

In closing, I stand ready to support you in improving your teaching performance, but that improvement clearly rests with you. Please contact my secretary to schedule a meeting if you wish to discuss this memorandum of concerns. At this meeting, you may be represented by a teachers' association representative or other person of your choice.

ABC SCHOOL DISTRICT   **KENNEDY ELEMENTARY SCHOOL**

1584 South Pineview Drive
Crescent Ridge, California 70799
(916) 444-4444

DATE: November 4, 20XX
TO: Mr. William Anthony
FROM: Dr. Lemmie Wade
RE: Memorandum of Concerns 2

This is the second memorandum of concerns sent to you with regard to the effectiveness of your teaching. I will state my concerns and offer suggestions to improve your teaching performance. Although you have shown some improvement, you must address classroom management and improve your teaching strategies so that effective learning will occur in your classroom.

Concern 1—Having an Unattractive Classroom

As stated earlier, I am concerned about the appearance of your classroom. A bulletin board should be changed periodically to reflect the seasons as well as to display successful schoolwork.

Suggestions

1. Use attractive colors on the bulletin boards to reflect the fall season.
2. Display schoolwork of your children.
3. Remove pencil and crayon marks from desks and floors.
4. Post your classroom management plan on a bulletin board.
5. Develop a procedure for cleaning the floor of paper and trash.

Concern 2—Ineffective Teaching Strategies

Suggestions

1. Develop lesson plans for each subject area.
2. Design your plan in a clear, logical, and sequential format.
3. To capture the students' attention, begin the lesson with a motivational activity.
4. Make the objective of the lesson known to students.
5. Maintain good momentum (pacing) to keep students involved.
6. Use a variety of questioning levels and give students ample opportunity to respond.
7. Check periodically for student comprehension of concepts.
8. Be more mobile in the classroom and do not stand in one location.
9. Use examples that students can understand.
10. Keep students involved in the lesson.
11. Reinforce appropriate student behavior.

12. Provide challenging seatwork related to the subject area being learned.
13. Make a smooth transition between activities.
14. Praise students for good work.
15. Use a variety of teaching strategies.
16. Develop a procedure for students to signal you when they need help.
17. Develop procedures for students who finish their work early.
18. Develop procedures for assigning students to cooperative groups.

In closing, I want you to know that I support you as a classroom teacher, but the responsibility to improve your teaching clearly rests with you. Because of the importance of this matter, we must meet to discuss this memorandum of concerns and to outline a specific time line for improvements to occur in your classroom. Please see my secretary to arrange a date and time for this meeting. At this meeting, you may be represented by a teachers' association representative or other person of your choice.

ABC SCHOOL DISTRICT   **KENNEDY ELEMENTARY SCHOOL**

1584 South Pineview Drive
Crescent Ridge, California 70799
(916) 444-4444

October 7, 20XX

Mr. William Anthony
Kennedy Elementary School

Dear Mr. Anthony:

Because it is important for you to improve your teaching performance, especially classroom management, I would like you to visit Mr. Scott Larson's classroom to observe classroom management procedures and instructional techniques in small and large group instruction.

Arrangements have been made for a substitute to teach your class on Monday, October 11, 20XX, from 9:30 to 11:00 A.M.

Again, I stand ready to assist you in making this school year a successful teaching experience.

Sincerely,

Lemmie Wade, PhD
Principal

Enclosure

ABC SCHOOL DISTRICT　　　　　**KENNEDY ELEMENTARY SCHOOL**

1584 South Pineview Drive
Crescent Ridge, California 70799
(916) 444-4444

December 3, 20XX

Mr. William Anthony
Kennedy Elementary School

Dear Mr. Anthony:

Because it is important for you to improve your teaching performance, especially classroom management, I would like you to visit Mr. Scott Larson's classroom.

I have made arrangements for a substitute to teach your class on Monday, December 13, 20XX, from 10:00 to 11:30 A.M.

During your observation, please use the enclosed form as a guide to comment about Mr. Larson's rules, procedures, and routines pertaining to classroom organization and management; instructional grouping strategies; and methods for closing the lesson and transitioning to the next lesson.

We will discuss your observation during our next conference.

Again, I stand ready to assist you in making this school year a successful teaching experience.

Sincerely,

Lemmie Wade, PhD
Principal

KENNEDY ELEMENTARY SCHOOL
PEER OBSERVATION FORM

Date _____ Time of Day _____ Class Period _____
Teacher Observing _____ Teacher Teaching _____

A. Starting the School Day
    1. How did the teacher escort students to the classroom?
    2. How did the teacher greet the students?
    3. What communication took place between the teacher and students? (Is it positive or negative, friendly or neutral, personal or general, etc.?)
    4. What opening school day activities occurred in the classroom? Were they planned or on-the-spot decisions? Were the activities work or fun? Was a time limit set?
    5. How did the teacher take attendance? (Using the seating chart? By homework turned in? Other?)
    6. How did the teacher collect money (lunch/supply/field trip)?

B. Classroom Instruction
    1. Did the teacher begin the lesson with a motivational activity to capture students' attention?
    2. Did the teacher make the objective known to students?
    3. How was the instructional material presented?
    4. How did the teacher begin the lesson quickly?
    5. What was the level of student participation?
    6. How did the teacher keep the students motivated during the lesson?
    7. How did the teacher use good examples?
    8. How did the teacher use a variety of questions?
    9. How mobile was the teacher? Did the teacher stand in one location or move around?
    10. Did the teacher's position affect discipline?

C. Lesson Closure
    1. How did the teacher close the lesson?
    2. How was completed work collected?
    3. How did the teacher assign homework?

D. Classroom Management
    1. What were the teacher's classroom management plans?
    2. What classroom management strategies were used to operate the classroom?
    3. What features reflected the teacher's enthusiasm (i.e., vocal delivery, eye movement, gestures, body movement, facial expression, word selection, acceptance of ideas and feelings, and overall energy)?

VI-B

E. Observation Conclusions
1. How did the teacher end the lesson?
2. How do you think the lesson went?
3. Did learning take place? How do you know?
4. Was discipline a problem?
5. What strategies did the teacher use that could help you improve your teaching?
6. What worked well? What did not work well?
7. What insights have you gained from observing this teacher?

ABC SCHOOL DISTRICT   **KENNEDY ELEMENTARY SCHOOL**

1584 South Pineview Drive
Crescent Ridge, California 70799
(916) 444-4444

October 12, 20XX

Mr. William Anthony
Kennedy Elementary School

Dear Mr. Anthony:

As we have discussed earlier, opportunities are available for teachers to observe classes in other schools in our district. Therefore I have arranged for you to spend a day at Redwood Elementary School, which is located at 8439 West Redwood Drive.

You are to report to the school office to meet with Mrs. Beverly Martinez, Principal at Redwood School, at 8:00 A.M. on Tuesday, October 19, 20XX. You will spend the entire day in the 5th grade classroom of Mr. David Riley. Mr. Riley is an experienced teacher who has excellent classroom management skills as well as instructional techniques. If you believe it would be worthwhile, I can arrange to have Mr. Riley visit your classroom, too.

Again, I stand ready to assist you in making this a successful teaching experience.

Sincerely,

Lemmie Wade, PhD
Principal

ABC SCHOOL DISTRICT   **KENNEDY ELEMENTARY SCHOOL**

1584 South Pineview Drive
Crescent Ridge, California 70799
(916) 444-4444

October 15, 20XX

Mr. William Anthony
Kennedy Elementary School

Dear Mr. Anthony:

I was pleased that your visit to Redwood Elementary School was a worthwhile professional development experience for you. Because I want to continue assisting you in improving your teaching performance, I have made arrangements for Mr. David Riley, a 5th grade teacher from Redwood Elementary School, to spend the entire school day in your classroom on Monday, October 25, 20XX. During that time, Mr. Riley will work with you in the following areas:

- Classroom management
- Reading instruction
- General organization

Again, I stand ready to assist you in making this school year a successful teaching experience.

Sincerely,

Lemmie Wade, PhD
Principal

ABC SCHOOL DISTRICT   **KENNEDY ELEMENTARY SCHOOL**

1584 South Pineview Drive
Crescent Ridge, California 70799
(916) 444-4444

September 23, 20XX

Mr. William Anthony
Kennedy Elementary School

Dear Mr. Anthony:

At the beginning of the school year, you received a copy of The Kennedy Elementary School Teachers' Handbook. This handbook is designed to provide information that will clarify rules and procedures to ensure the smooth operation of our school. Teachers are responsible for knowing the information contained in the handbook and are expected to observe all procedures therein. The handbook sections listed include critical information that will help you improve your teaching performance. Please review the following sections:

Section	Title
IV	Effective Instructional Strategies
V	School Procedures
VI	Classroom Management

I stand ready to assist you in making this a successful school year.

Sincerely,

Lemmie Wade, PhD
Principal

Enclosures—Teachers' Handbook Overview and Table of Contents

(NOTE: Include a copy of the pages cited in the handbook when preparing the Unsatisfactory Teacher Evaluation Document.)

KENNEDY ELEMENTARY SCHOOL

TEACHERS' HANDBOOK

20XX-20XX SCHOOL YEAR

TEACHERS' HANDBOOK OVERVIEW

The Kennedy Elementary School Teachers' Handbook is organized into six sections and provides information regarding rules, policies, procedures, and overall operation of the school. Section I contains the school calendar, schedule of events for the school year, and a school directory. Section II contains the school philosophy, including mission statement, and goals and objectives. Section III provides information about Kennedy's administration and staff, school statistics, and the operational process for school decisions. Section IV explains the school curriculum, instructional strategies, lesson planning, and classroom management. Section V contains information about school procedures, such as fire, tornado, crisis, and in-school safety drills. Section VI focuses on classroom management and contains strategies used by effective classroom teachers. This section provides a list of class discipline problems and the strategies that teachers can use to reduce classroom disruptions. Section VII provides information on procedures for staff performance evaluations.

TABLE OF CONTENTS

A message from the principal

Visitors to building
Volunteers' job descriptions
Acceptable staff behavior
Tips to reduce staff/student conflict
Confidentiality of records
Student attendance
Lockers
Grading
School safety
After school detention
Extra curricular activities
Dress code
Homework policy
Health records
Cumulative folders
Health and special education students
Promotion/retention policy

Section VI: Classroom Management
Discipline policy of district and school
Classroom organization
Classroom rules
School rules
School district rules
Student discipline
Student referral procedures

Section VII: Staff Evaluation
Teachers
Specialists
Educational assistants

Appendix

ABC SCHOOL DISTRICT   **KENNEDY ELEMENTARY SCHOOL**

1584 South Pineview Drive
Crescent Ridge, California 70799
(916) 444-4444

October 22, 20XX

Mr. William Anthony
Kennedy Elementary School

Dear Mr. Anthony:

Enclosed you will find copies of the following articles, which should help you improve your classroom management and teaching techniques:

1. "Proactive Classroom Strategies for the Urban School Setting"
2. "Basic Classroom Management"

As always, I stand ready to assist you in making this school year a successful teaching experience.

Sincerely,

Lemmie Wade, PhD
Principal

Enclosures

(NOTE: Include a copy of the articles when preparing the Unsatisfactory Teacher Evaluation Document.)

ABC SCHOOL DISTRICT   **KENNEDY ELEMENTARY SCHOOL**

1584 South Pineview Drive
Crescent Ridge, California 70799
(916) 444-4444

November 16, 20XX

Mr. William Anthony
Kennedy Elementary School

Dear Mr. Anthony:

Enclosed you will find copies of the following articles, which should help you improve your classroom management and teaching techniques:

1. "Creating a Positive Classroom Learning Experience"
2. "How to Prepare an Effective Reading Lesson"
3. "Discipline—A Step-by-Step Guide for Elementary School Teachers"

As always, I stand ready to assist you in making this school year a successful teaching experience.

Sincerely,

Lemmie Wade, PhD
Principal

Enclosures

(NOTE: Include a copy of the articles when preparing the Unsatisfactory Teacher Evaluation Document.)

ABC SCHOOL DISTRICT   **KENNEDY ELEMENTARY SCHOOL**

1584 South Pineview Drive
Crescent Ridge, California 70799
(916) 444-4444

December 7, 20XX

Mr. William Anthony
Kennedy Elementary School

Dear Mr. Anthony:

Enclosed you will find copies of the following articles, which should help you improve your classroom management and teaching techniques:

1. "A Word of Caution on the Use of Reward Systems in the Classroom"
2. "Manipulatives and Mathematics"
3. "Essentials of Lesson Plan Design"

As always, I stand ready to assist you in making this school year a successful teaching experience.

Sincerely,

Lemmie Wade, PhD
Principal

Enclosures

(NOTE: Include a copy of the articles when preparing the Unsatisfactory Teacher Evaluation Document.)

ABC SCHOOL DISTRICT   **KENNEDY ELEMENTARY SCHOOL**

1584 South Pineview Drive
Crescent Ridge, California 70799
(916) 444-4444

October 20, 20XX

Mr. William Anthony
Kennedy Elementary School

Dear Mr. Anthony:

The ABC School District Staff Development Bulletin, Fall 20XX, lists several inservice classes that should be beneficial in improving your classroom teaching performance. I suggest that you enroll in the following classes:

- Classroom Management
- Teaching Reading in the Intermediate Grades
- Cooperative Learning

Registration forms are available in the school office.

As always, I stand ready to assist you in making this a successful teaching experience.

Sincerely,

Lemmie Wade, PhD
Principal

Enclosures

(NOTE: Include a copy of the pages from the bulletin when preparing the Unsatisfactory Teacher Evaluation Document.)

ABC SCHOOL DISTRICT   **KENNEDY ELEMENTARY SCHOOL**

1584 South Pineview Drive
Crescent Ridge, California 70799
(916) 444-4444

December 15, 20XX

Mr. William Anthony
Kennedy Elementary School

Dear Mr. Anthony:

The ABC School District Staff Development Bulletin, Spring 20XX, lists several inservice classes that would be beneficial in improving your classroom teaching performance. I suggest that you enroll in the following classes:

- Reading in the Content Areas
- Assertive Discipline
- Survival Skills for the Classroom Teacher

Registration forms are available in the school office.

As always, I stand ready to assist you in making this a successful teaching experience.

Sincerely,

Lemmie Wade, PhD
Principal

Enclosures

(NOTE: Include a copy of the pages from the bulletin when preparing the Unsatisfactory Teacher Evaluation Document.)

ABC SCHOOL DISTRICT   **KENNEDY ELEMENTARY SCHOOL**

1584 South Pineview Drive
Crescent Ridge, California 70799
(916) 444-4444

November 2, 20XX

Mr. William Anthony
Kennedy Elementary School

Dear Mr. Anthony:

The ABC Teachers' Convention is scheduled to be held from November 4 to 5, 20XX, at the Metropolitan Convention Center.

The convention booklet lists several workshops that should assist you in improving your teaching performance. I suggest that you attend the following workshops:

Title	Date	Time	Room
Conflict Resolution	11/4/XX	9:30 A.M.	Renaissance
Classroom Management	11/4/XX	11:00 A.M.	Van Gogh
New Instructional Strategies	11/4/XX	2:30 P.M.	Rembrandt
Cooperative Learning	11/5/XX	9:30 A.M.	Van Gogh
Multicultural Awareness	11/5/XX	11:00 A.M.	Renaissance
Assertive Discipline	11/5/XX	2:30 P.M.	Van Gogh

As always, I stand ready to assist you in making this school year a successful teaching experience.

Sincerely,

Lemmie Wade, PhD
Principal

ABC SCHOOL DISTRICT   **KENNEDY ELEMENTARY SCHOOL**

1584 South Pineview Drive
Crescent Ridge, California 70799
(916) 444-4444

October 14, 20XX

Mr. William Anthony
Kennedy Elementary School

Dear Mr. Anthony:

Although you were previously given several suggestions to improve your teaching performance, I am providing you with a copy of the videotape series, "A Proactive Approach to Positive Classroom Management," which shows successful classroom management techniques. I would like for you to review these tapes and then meet with me to discuss the incorporation of these techniques into your classroom management. Please see my secretary to schedule a meeting with me.

Sincerely,

Lemmie Wade, PhD
Principal

Enclosure

ABC SCHOOL DISTRICT   **KENNEDY ELEMENTARY SCHOOL**

1584 South Pineview Drive
Crescent Ridge, California 70799
(916) 444-4444

October 22, 20XX

Mr. William Anthony
Kennedy Elementary School

Dear Mr. Anthony:

As a resource for classroom teachers, a series of videotapes was recently purchased by our school district, which features Dr. Nikolus Jones, who is one of the leading experts in the field of education. The series offers excellent information that should help you become a more effective teacher. Therefore I suggest that you view them in the school library within the next week:

1. The Effective Teacher (30 minutes)
2. Lesson Planning (25 minutes)
3. Effective Classroom Management (30 minutes)
4. Classroom Rules and Procedures (28 minutes)
5. Key Instructional Behaviors (35 minutes)

At our next postobservation conference, plan to discuss new strategies that you gleaned from these videotapes.

I stand ready to assist you in making this a successful school year.

Sincerely,

Lemmie Wade, PhD
Principal

ABC SCHOOL DISTRICT **KENNEDY ELEMENTARY SCHOOL**

1584 South Pineview Drive
Crescent Ridge, California 70799
(916) 444-4444

November 10, 20XX

Mr. William Anthony
Kennedy Elementary School

Dear Mr. Anthony:

I am providing you with a copy of the following videotapes, which show successful classroom management techniques:

- "Increasing Student Achievement through Cooperative Learning"
- "Creating an Atmosphere for Positive Student Interaction"

I would like for you to review these tapes and then meet with me to discuss the incorporation of these techniques in your classroom. Please see my secretary to schedule a meeting with me.

Sincerely,

Lemmie Wade, PhD
Principal

Enclosures

ABC SCHOOL DISTRICT   **KENNEDY ELEMENTARY SCHOOL**

1584 South Pineview Drive
Crescent Ridge, California 70799
(916) 444-4444

December 8, 20XX

Mr. William Anthony
Kennedy Elementary School

Dear Mr. Anthony:

I am providing you with a copy of the following videotape, which shows successful classroom management techniques:

- "Structuring the Classroom Environment for Large Group, Small Group, and Individualized Instruction"

I would like for you to review this tape and then meet with me to discuss the incorporation of these techniques in your classroom. Please see my secretary to schedule a meeting with me.

Sincerely,

Lemmie Wade, PhD
Principal

Enclosure

ABC SCHOOL DISTRICT

KENNEDY ELEMENTARY SCHOOL

1584 South Pineview Drive
Crescent Ridge, California 70799
(916) 444-4444

October 22, 20XX

Mr. William Anthony
Kennedy Elementary School

Dear Mr. Anthony:

As you know, our school is connected to the Internet through the district's Technology Department. Several World Wide Web (WWW) sites are available for teachers. I would like you to explore the following Web sites dealing with effective teaching strategies:

> http://www.effectiveteaching.com
> http://www.classroomdiscipline.com
> http://www.assertivediscipline.com
> http://www.modelsofdiscipline.com
> http://www.goodteachersdo.com
> http://www.lessonplans.com

I have heard many positive comments from teachers about these Web sites and believe they will help you improve your teaching. The lesson plans site provides lesson plans that are organized by grade level and subject areas.

Sincerely,

Lemmie Wade, PhD
Principal

ABC SCHOOL DISTRICT   **KENNEDY ELEMENTARY SCHOOL**

1584 South Pineview Drive
Crescent Ridge, California 70799
(916) 444-4444

November 4, 20XX

Mr. William Anthony
Kennedy Elementary School

Dear Mr. Anthony:

In addition to the Web sites that I listed in my October 22, 20XX, letter to you, I suggest that you log on to National Teacher Talk, which is specifically designed for classroom teachers to discuss and share classroom issues. The Web site address is http//www.teachertalk.com.

This is an excellent site to obtain information about classroom instruction and classroom management. In addition, the site offers message pages where you can leave specific questions for other teachers to answer.

If you have any questions about accessing this Web site, please contact me.

Sincerely,

Lemmie Wade, PhD
Principal

ABC SCHOOL DISTRICT   **KENNEDY ELEMENTARY SCHOOL**

1584 South Pineview Drive
Crescent Ridge, California 70799
(916) 444-4444

October 18, 20XX

Mr. William Anthony
Kennedy Elementary School

Dear Mr. Anthony:

Enclosed is a copy of the 20XX catalog from the McLeon Publishing Company for the 20XX-20XX school year. All classroom teachers are allocated funds to purchase supplies and books; you may want to use a portion of these funds to order some reference books that will help you improve your teaching.

If you are interested in purchasing any of these books, please follow the ordering procedures outlined in the teachers' handbook.

Sincerely,

Lemmie Wade, PhD
Principal

Enclosure

ABC SCHOOL DISTRICT   **KENNEDY ELEMENTARY SCHOOL**

1584 South Pineview Drive
Crescent Ridge, California 70799
(916) 444-4444

November 15, 20XX

Mr. William Anthony
Kennedy Elementary School

Dear Mr. Anthony:

As you know, the weekly staff bulletin is distributed at the end of the day on Friday. It is printed on goldenrod paper so that it easily stands out from other papers, and staff members know that it is important to read.

The bulletin contains information about daily school events for the next week and also has a monthly schedule of upcoming school activities. In addition to listing these events and activities, detailed information is provided, including the roll of staff members at these activities.

The four sections of the weekly bulletin are Good News Celebration, Daily Activities, Staff Checklist, and Looking Ahead. The tips in the checklist are suggestions for running an effective school (e.g., teachers are reminded to pick up their students on time and quietly escort them to their classrooms).

I want you to reread the Staff Checklist section in the weekly bulletins that have been distributed to date and continue to read future weekly bulletins throughout the remainder of the school year. This is valuable information that can help you improve your teaching performance.

Sincerely,

Lemmie Wade, PhD
Principal

Enclosures

(NOTE: Include a copy of the weekly bulletins when preparing the Unsatisfactory Teacher Evaluation Document.)

KENNEDY ELEMENTARY SCHOOL
WEEKLY BULLETIN
WEEK OF SEPTEMBER 6-10, 20XX

Good News Celebration!
- The chess team won the tournament.
- Happy birthday to Mr. Jones, our school engineer.
- Five teachers represented the school at the 5K Run at Lake Mead Park on Saturday.

Daily Activities

Monday, September 6
- New teacher meeting in the cafeteria at 8:05 A.M.
- Classes delayed 10 minutes to take attendance (from 9:00-9:10 A.M.).
- Staff meeting in the library at 3:15 P.M.

Tuesday, September 7
- Leadership council meeting in the library at 8:05 A.M.
- Debate club meeting in Room 36 at 3:00 P.M.
- Dance troupe practice after school in the gym.

Wednesday, September 8

Thursday, September 9
- School committee meetings in designated rooms at 3:15 P.M.

Friday, September 10
- Payday

Staff Checklist
Assigned teachers and staff escort students to and from the cafeteria.
Teachers enter "E" on the attendance sheet the day a student enrolls in your room.
All staff review fire drill procedures.
Looking Ahead to September Activities
    9/14/XX (Tuesday) 3:15 P.M. Staff meeting in the library
    9/16/XX (Thursday) 8:00 A.M. New teacher meeting in Room 15
    9/21/XX (Tuesday 6:30 P.M. School Leadership Meeting in the library

ABC SCHOOL DISTRICT

KENNEDY ELEMENTARY SCHOOL

1584 South Pineview Drive
Crescent Ridge, California 70799
(916) 444-4444

September 14, 20XX

Mr. William Anthony
Kennedy Elementary School

Dear Mr. Anthony:

This is the third week of the school year, and I am concerned about what appears to be a lack of procedures in your classroom. When I observed your classroom yesterday, I was uncertain that students knew your procedures. Please take time to describe your procedures for the following basic classroom activities:

A. Beginning Class
   1. Taking and recording attendance/tardiness
   2. Providing academic warm-ups
   3. Distributing materials
   4. Beginning the lesson
   5. Gaining students' attention

B. Use of Classroom/School Areas
   1. Drinks, bathroom, pencil sharpener
   2. Student storage
   3. Learning centers
   4. Playground/school grounds

C. Work Requirements/Procedures
   1. Paper heading
   2. Use of pen or pencil
   3. Writing on the back of paper
   4. Neatness/legibility
   5. Incomplete work
   6. Late work
   7. Missed work
   8. Independent work
   9. Definition of "working alone"
   10. Passing out books/supplies
   11. Movement in and out of small groups
   12. Expected behavior in groups
   13. Out-of-seat policies
   14. Talking among students (general and during seatwork)
   15. Conduct during interruptions

VI-M

16. Homework assignments
17. Collecting assignments
18. Marking/grading papers
19. Returning assignments
20. Posting student work
21. Rewards and incentives

Plan to complete your response and forward it to me by September 20, 20XX

Sincerely,

Lemmie Wade, PhD
Principal

ABC SCHOOL DISTRICT   **KENNEDY ELEMENTARY SCHOOL**

1584 South Pineview Drive
Crescent Ridge, California 70799
(916) 444-4444

November 12, 20XX

Mr. William Anthony
Kennedy Elementary School

Dear Mr. Anthony:

During the past 10 weeks, I have made suggestions to help you improve your teaching performance in the following areas:

- *Classroom Organization and Procedures*
  Physical organization
  Expectations
  Grading system

- *Learning Environment*
  Positive teacher-student interaction
  Rewards and encouragement
  Multicultural awareness

- *Lesson Planning and Presentation*
  Introduction
  Motivation
  Organization
  Closure
  Assessment

- *Instructional Techniques*
  Cooperative learning
  Reading instruction
  Mathematics instruction

- *Student Discipline*
  Conflict resolution
  Assertive discipline

I would like to meet with you to discuss these suggestions for improvement and the progress that you have made. Please contact my secretary to schedule an appointment with me.

As always, I stand ready to assist you in making this school year a successful teaching experience.

Sincerely,

Lemmie Wade, PhD
Principal

ABC SCHOOL DISTRICT

KENNEDY ELEMENTARY SCHOOL

1584 South Pineview Drive
Crescent Ridge, California 70799
(916) 444-4444

The following disciplinary referrals from Mr. William Anthony were sent to me to resolve.

Date	Time	Comments	Recommendations	Disposition
9-6-XX	8:25	Disrupts class with yelling and pounding on desk.	Return student when ready to return.	Counseled and returned to class.
9-6-XX	8:37	Refuses to leave other children alone during reading class by yelling across the room.	Return student when ready to return.	Discussed appropriate behavior with student. Detained until music class.
9-6-XX	8:53	Throwing pencil on floor and refuses to work.	Refer to guidance counselor.	Detained.
9-6-XX	9:10	In the hall without shoes kicking other children.	None	Escorted student to class to get shoes.
9-6-XX	10:30	Crawling around room and refusing to sit in assigned seat.	Return student when ready to return.	Detained.
9-8-XX	10:25	Throwing paper on the floor and walking around the room. Stopping others from learning.	None	Counseled and called parent.
9-10-XX	None	Crawling on floor and using profane language.	None	Referred to counselor.
9-10-XX	None	Throwing pencils on floor. Refuses to be quiet.	Maintain child in office until prepared to work with teacher.	Detained 30 minutes.

Date	Time	Comments	Recommendations	Disposition
9-12-XX	10:20	Refuses to be quiet and work.	Return to class when ready to be quiet and follow directions of teacher.	Counseled and returned.
9-12-XX	10:40	Refuses to work this morning.	Maintain in office.	Student ill. Called mother to pick up student.
9-12-XX	11:10	Very loud in class by using foul language.	None	Detained.
9-13-XX	10:35	Child is creating a safety problem by throwing crayons.	Keep child in office until ready to cooperate with teacher.	Detained.
9-14-XX	None	Walking around the room hitting other children.	Told child about class rules about keeping hands to themselves.	Counseled about expected behavior.
9-15-XX	11:30	Writing on the floor with crayon and throwing them around the room.	Told to write rule about throwing things in class.	Counseled. Student to wash crayons off the floor.
9-16-XX	1:00	Banging on desk with a pencil. Refuses to follow the instructions of the teacher.	None	Called parent and returned to class.
9-17-XX	1:25	Using profane language in class.	I called parent last night to inform them of poor use of words by their child.	Called parent. Returned to class.
10-5-XX	10:00	Crawling around on the floor for about 20 minutes.	Return to class when able to be quiet.	Counseled and returned.
10-8-XX	10:35	Hitting other children in class.	Detention assigned for this noon.	Detained during lunch.
10-22-XX	11:40	Refuses to stop screaming across room.	Detention assigned for this noon.	Detained during lunch.
10-25-XX	9:35	Fighting in the classroom.	None	Referred to peer mediation.

VII

Date	Time	Comments	Recommendations	Disposition
10-26-XX	None	Refuses to line up to enter the building.	None	Returned. Needs to practice procedures.
10-26-XX	1:30	Yelling during social studies.	None	Counseled and returned to class after recess.
11-5-XX	9:40	Yelling out during reading period.	Maintain in class until able to not disrupt this class reading.	Detained and counseled.
11-5-XX	9:55	Continues to disrupt class by walking around the room.	Keep out class for duration of class period.	Referred to psychologist.
11-5-XX	11:10	Talking out in class.	Keep for the hour.	Detained and counseled.
11-5-XX	1:15	Yelling in class.	Keep for the class period.	Talked about proper behavior in class.
11-5-XX	1:45	Running and kicking. Throwing things in class.	None	Counseled.
11-8-XX	2:50	Refuses to be quiet and work. Reading group cannot be held with this disruption.	Keep for reading period.	Detained.
11-8-XX	2:50	Swearing in class.	Keep for the morning.	Counseled. Sent letter to parent for conference.
11-9-XX	10:15	Throwing books around the room.	Keep for the morning.	Counseled and detained.
11-9-XX	11:45	Fighting in the classroom.	Call parent and suspend.	Suspended. Picked up by father.
11-17-XX	11:15	Walking on top of tables and yelling in class.	Detain for the hour.	Detained until the end of lunch.
12-6-XX	10:25	Calls out and disrupts class. Pounds desk. He has work and continues to disrupt.	Return pink slip when student returns.	Detained and counseled.

Date	Time	Comments	Recommendations	Disposition
12-6-XX	None	Refuses to leave _____ alone. Her parents will call police. Threatens to hit her. Yells across the room.	Psychologist needs to counsel. Please return pink slip before he returns.	Detained and talked to _____!
12-6-XX	None	No supplies. Throws loaned pencil on floor. Sits in wrong seat. Refuses to work.	Refer to psychologist for help and guidance.	Retained by _____. Sees the psychologist on 12-7-XX (P.M.)
12-6-XX	9:10	____was brought in from the playground with _____. He had kicked ____on the lip with his foot. _____was bleeding on his lip. The aide left both of them in Rm. 27.	None	Students were told to stand quietly until they behaved. Counseled.
12-6-XX	10:30	Crawls around room. Refuses to sit or work on easiest things. Daily, hourly disruption.	Return pink slip with her.	Student was told to stand quietly until he behaved.
12-8-XX	10:25	Calls out. Throws coloring paper on floor. Breaks pencils purposely. Walks around and refuses to sit. Prevents others from learning.	None	_____was told how she should behave. She was told to stand until she was ready to do some work.
12-10-XX	None	Told to sit down more than three times. Crawls on floor. Bad language to____. Kicks____. Stole_____pencil. Safety hazard to other students.	None	Detention. Letter to parent.
12-10-XX	None	Chronic lack of supplies. Throws crayons on floors. Told to be quiet four times and refuses.	Keep out until ready to do class work.	Counseled and called mother this A.M.

VII

Date	Time	Comments	Recommendations	Disposition
12-13-XX	10:15	Says shut up to____. Refuses to sit and be quiet and work. Uncooperative.	Keep out until she can follow rules.	Ready to work. Detained.
12-13-XX	10:20	Even with _____ helping, he refuses to sit, be quiet, and work.	Return when he is willing to follow rules and let others learn.	Detained all day.
12-13-XX	11:10	Refuses to cooperate. Very loud. Won't sit down. Tries to hand out papers. Uses foul language (dick, gay, homo). A regular circus clown. Thinks she's very funny.	None	Parent conference held.
12-14-XX	10:35	Throws crayons. Refuses to cooperate with _____who is trying to give help. Safety hazard. Throws crayons.	Keep out until ready to behave.	Ready to work.
12-14-XX	1:15	Walked across room and hit _____ in the face at 1:00. _____ was in his seat.	Must know he can't hit other students here!	Counseled and detained.
12-15-XX	11:30	Wrote on floor with crayon. Flips crayons around the room. Kicks _____. Won't sit. Needs to be held by adult to be quiet. Mother was called at 10:30 by _____.	No V.I.P. Program. Return when willing to be quiet, sit, and work.	Detained until 1:25 P.M.
12-16-XX	1:00	Bangs on desk. Doesn't sit. Safety hazard. Will break neck or leg on desk. Refused to settle down. Needs one adult to sit with him at all times.	Return when quiet, sits down and works.	Detained until 3:35 P.M.

Date	Time	Comments	Recommendations	Disposition
12-17-XX	1:25	Inappropriate language (kiss your mother's wiener) to _____. Scribbles on desk. Calls out. Doesn't work. _____hit him.	Parent be called. Explain to parent his language and poor behavior.	Detention and written task. Message re: parent telephone request.
1-5-XX	10:00	Refuses to work. Throws work on floor. Crawls on floor. Samples of 45 worksheets stapled to this.	Return when able to be quiet.	Ready to return at 1:10 P.M.
1-10-XX	None	She entered building at 12:50. Hit several students despite being told to keep her hands to herself. Tipped her chair over. Refused to settle down.	Detention at noon. Call parent.	Detained.
1-21-XX	11:40	Yells across room. ____threatens___ & ____"if you want her to live." Tries to get_____to beat up the two girls. Told to do own work. Across the room he refuses to leave ____and___alone.	Detention at noon. Call mother at home. Continual problem.	Detained P.M.
1-24-XX	9:35	No crayons, erasers. No effort to work.	None	Ready to return.
1-24-XX	11:00	Ran down hall. Didn't go to toilet. Disobedient. Calls out. Disrupts constantly. Put plastic bag over her head.	Detain until able to be non-disruptive.	Going home with mother's consent.

VII

Date	Time	Comments	Recommendations	Disposition
1-24-XX	1:30	We were learning tens in math. _____had difficulty. She yelled, threw her paper on the floor, and crayons down. Refused to settle down.	Call mother. Tantrums not needed at school.	Detained until 2:30 P.M.
2-4-XX	9:50	Hit and kicked ____. Yells out to reading group. Prevents the class from learning to read. Disrespectful.	Call parent. Keep out until able to not disrupt this class reading.	Returned to class 10:25 A.M.
12-4-XX	9:55	Repeatedly told to work. Continues to talk across room and does not work. Prevents education and reading groups from operating.	Keep out until ready for class and work.	Ready to work (10:25 A.M.).
2-4-XX	1:10	Prevents reading work of class being improved. Gets up and rips_____work. Does not do as told.	Keep out until we can do reading groups.	Detained.
2-4-XX	1:45	Ran and kicked _____. Tossed out of library by aide. Refuses to write lines. Throws pencil on floor. Throws things.	None	Asked D.S. to keep him in room. She sent him to office.
2-4-XX	2:25	Yells out loud. Refuses to listen to art teacher. Disrespectful.	Keep out rest of day. Class deserves art.	Counseled and returned to class.
2-4-XX	2:50	Refuses to be quiet and work. Kicks ____. Group reading cannot be held with this disruption.	None	Detained.

VII

Date	Time	Comments	Recommendations	Disposition
2-4-XX	2:50	Rude. Kindergarten readiness. Does not work. Continual disrupter. Kicking_____still. Steals_____'s eraser.	Keep out.	Talked with_____. Referred to psychologist.
2-4-XX	10:15	Got out of seat and hit_____. Excuse was_____said "his momma." Refused to apologize. Belligerent. Threatens to punch _____or anyone's face through wall.	Keep out.	Counseled and detained. Returned at 11:15 A.M.
2-4-XX	None	Returned 11:30. Not ready for class. Belligerent still.	None	Detained.
2-7-XX	11:15	Calls out. Walks out of seat to hit _____two desks away. Constant noise. Prevents education of a class.	None	Detention.
2-7-XX	1:12	Prevents P.M. reading groups. Yells out. Talks. Told to be quiet four times.	Keep until quiet.	Counseled and detained.
2-7-XX	1:20	P.M. reading group disrupter. Loud, rude when not chosen to go with tutor.	Keep out all afternoon. Don't return today. Call social worker. Problem at home?	Detained P.M.
2-9-XX	11:05	Disrupts class. _____(parent) removed him.	None	Student detained.
2-9-XX	11:05	Disrupts class. _____(parent) removed him.	None	Student detention.
2-9-XX	11:30	Not respectful to ___. Removed by___.	Call parent.	Student detained.

VII

Date	Time	Comments	Recommendations	Disposition
2-9-XX	1:30	Removed by_____.	Call parent.	Student detention.
2-21-XX	1:30	At 9:10 he had some candy stolen by someone in Room 30. He has been upset and uncooperative all day. He is unwilling to work or act decently in the room.	Keep out rest of day.	Detained.
2-21-XX	None	Refuses to settle down after lunch indoors. Does not sit. Ripped_____'s work.	Keep out one hour at least. Call parent.	Called parent and detained.
2-22-XX	9:45	Refuses to keep reader open. Does not want to learn to read.	Call parent. Bad attitude. Disrupts the perfect group and great room.	Counseled and returned.

ABC SCHOOL DISTRICT   **KENNEDY ELEMENTARY SCHOOL**

1584 South Pineview Drive
Crescent Ridge, California 70799
(916) 444-4444

During the 20XX-20XX school year, parental complaints were registered at Kennedy Elementary School against William Anthony. These 23 parental complaints were related to the teacher's performance and its negative impact on student learning. The ABC School District procedures were followed in resolving these parental complaints. At this time, I will give you a brief overview of the nature of these parental complaints, including letters and telephone messages.

VIII

ABC SCHOOL DISTRICT   **KENNEDY ELEMENTARY SCHOOL**

1584 South Pineview Drive
Crescent Ridge, California 70799
(916) 444-4444

September 10, 20XX

Mr. William Anthony
Kennedy Elementary School

Dear Mr. Anthony:

Part III, Section A, of the ABC School District Contract states that, when parental or public complaints are filed, the individual teacher must be made aware of the complaint. Therefore I am forwarding the attached letter/parental complaint form received about you on September 9, 20XX.

Please plan to meet in my office on September 12, 20XX, at 3:15 P.M. to discuss this parental complaint. If this time is inconvenient, please contact my secretary to reschedule the meeting. We must resolve this complaint by September 14, 20XX.

Sincerely,

Lemmie Wade, PhD
Principal

Enclosure

KENNEDY ELEMENTARY SCHOOL PARENTAL COMPLAINT FORM

Date _____   Time _____ A.M./P.M.

Student _____   Grade _____ ID Number _____

Address _____

Person Filing Complaint _____

Relationship to Student _____

Phone Number: Home _____   Other _____

Nature of Complaint _____
_____
_____
_____

Action Requested _____
_____

Has a Previous Complaint Been Filed? Yes _____ No _____ Date(s) _____

Person(s) Spoken with:

_____
Name/Title/Department

_____
Name/Title/Department

Resolution _____
_____
_____
_____
_____

Complaint Resolved _____ Further Action Necessary _____

_____   _____
Signature/Title   Date

September 15, 20XX

Dear Mrs. Wade, Principal:

I am writing this letter to inform you that I am very concerned about the safety of my son who is in Mr. Anthony's room, Room 214. My son told me that there have been several instances of students being hit in the head with flying objects. In fact, my son has been hit two or three times with pencils and once with a wood cube. Also, a child who was imitating a TV wrestler tried to choke my son in class. In addition, my son told me that scissors are thrown across the room and spitballs fly pretty regularly.

My son comes home with headaches caused by the noise in the classroom and he doesn't want to go back to school anymore.

I am afraid for my son's safety as well as the safety of other children in Mr. Anthony's classroom. I believe that my son is not getting a good education.

Because I am concerned that my child may be hurt in Mr. Anthony's classroom, I am requesting that he be assigned immediately to Mr. Patterson's class.

Sincerely,

Mrs. Johnson

September 15, 20XX

To Whom It May Concern:

I am afraid for my daughter Judy in Mr. Anthony's classroom, Room 214. My daughter is afraid of being hit with spitballs, crayons, and other flying objects in the classroom. She says that Mr. Anthony stands in front of the classroom and doesn't pay attention to the bad children throwing things in class. She also says that her school supplies (paper, pencils, pens, markers, and crayons) have been stolen out of her desk. Judy does not want to go back to Mr. Anthony's classroom.

Sincerely,

Mrs. Reyes

Mrs. Wade,

Are children out of control in Room 214? My son Johnny says his classroom is out of control and no learning is taking place. If this is true, I want him transferred to another classroom immediately. Johnny also says that Mr. Anthony doesn't have any control over the children. He does not want to go back to school if he has to go to Mr. Anthony's classroom.

Please call me at 775-8339 to let me know about your decision to transfer my son to another classroom. I want to hear from you by the end of this week or I will take this to the media. I want something done.

Mr. John Zebelle, Sr.

KENNEDY ELEMENTARY SCHOOL

To: *Dr. Wade*

Date: *9/17/20XX*   TIME: *11:45 A.M.*

While you were out

Mrs. Beverly Rodriguez

Parent of

_____

Phone   *897-4000 Ex. 35*

Telephoned	☒
Came to see you	☐
Wants to see you	☐
Please call him/her	☒
Will call again	☐
Urgent	☐
Returned your call	☐

Message Re: *Mr. Anthony's classroom.*
Wants her son transferred to another room.

KENNEDY ELEMENTARY SCHOOL

To: *Dr. Wade*

Date: *10/7/20XX* TIME: *10:30* A.M.
2:30 P.M.

While you were out

Mr. and Mrs. Simmons

Parent of

Phone *303-9393*

Telephoned	☒
Came to see you	☐
Wants to see you	☐
Please call him/her	☒
Will call again	☒
Urgent	☐
Returned your call	☐

Message Re: *Mr. Anthony's classroom.*
Wants their daughter transferred to another room.
This is the second message.

VIII-C5

KENNEDY ELEMENTARY SCHOOL

To: *Dr. Wade*

Date: *10/7/20XX*   TIME: *10:30 A.M.*
                                       11:20 A.M.

While you were out

Ms. Henderson

of

Parent Complaint Center
_____

Phone   *444-9705*

Telephoned	☒
Came to see you	☐
Wants to see you	☐
Please call him/her	☐
Will call again	☐
Urgent	☒
Returned your call	☐

Message Re: *Mr. and Mrs. Simmons. They are complaining about a teacher at school—Mr. Anthony.*

KENNEDY ELEMENTARY SCHOOL

To: *Dr. Wade*

Date: *10/8/20XX*   TIME: *8:00 A.M.*

While you were out

Board Member Fowler

of

ABC School District
_____

Phone   *498-3042*

Telephoned	☒
Came to see you	☐
Wants to see you	☐
Please call him/her	☒
Will call again	☐
Urgent	☒
Returned your call	☐

Message *Wants to know when you are transferring Johnny to another classroom.*

VIII-C7

ABC SCHOOL DISTRICT   **KENNEDY ELEMENTARY SCHOOL**

1584 South Pineview Drive
Crescent Ridge, California 70799
(916) 444-4444

Attached are samples of work given to students by Mr. William Anthony.

ABC SCHOOL DISTRICT   **KENNEDY ELEMENTARY SCHOOL**

1584 South Pineview Drive
Crescent Ridge, California 70799
(916) 444-4444

Attached are unsatisfactory evaluation letters issued concerning Mr. William Anthony's teaching performance.

X

ABC SCHOOL DISTRICT   **KENNEDY ELEMENTARY SCHOOL**

                                       1584 South Pineview Drive
                                       Crescent Ridge, California 70799
                                       (916) 444-4444

DATE: October 27, 20XX
TO: Dr. Derek Rodriguez, Director—Instructional Monitoring
FROM: Lemmie Wade, Principal
RE: POTENTIAL UNSATISFACTORY EVALUATION

During September and October 20XX, formal and informal observations were conducted in all teachers' classroom. I observed Mr. Anthony on

Day	Date	Time
Wednesday	September 8, 20XX	8:00-8:25 A.M.
Friday	September 10, 20XX	10:20-10:30 A.M.
Tuesday	September 14, 20XX	1:10-1:25 P.M.
Monday	September 20, 20XX	2:15-2:30 P.M.
Wednesday	September 22, 20XX	2:45-3:00 P.M.
Monday	September 27, 20XX	8:10-8:30 A.M.
Friday	October 1, 20XX	9:15-10:10 A.M.
Wednesday	October 6, 20XX	8:05-9:00 A.M.
Tuesday	October 12, 20XX	10:15-11:05 A.M.
Tuesday	October 19, 20XX	9:10-10:20 A.M.

These observations represent a reasonable sampling and included Mr. Anthony's assignment, morning and afternoon.

During the postobservation conferences, Mr. Anthony's strengths and weaknesses were discussed. In addition, I offered suggestions for improvement, described the assistance available, and set a reasonable period of time for necessary improvement.

Enclosed is a copy of the summary letter dated October 27, 20XX, and given to Mr. Anthony offering specific suggestions for improvement. Also enclosed are copies of the formal and informal observation/evaluation forms used to observe Mr. Anthony.

I have used the same formal and informal evaluation forms that were presented to all teachers on September 1, 20XX, with a letter explaining the evaluation process at Kennedy Elementary School.

cc: Calvin P. Thompson, Attorney at Law—ABC School District

Enclosures

ABC SCHOOL DISTRICT   **KENNEDY ELEMENTARY SCHOOL**

1584 South Pineview Drive
Crescent Ridge, California 70799
(916) 444-4444

DATE: November 23, 20XX
TO: Dr. Derek Rodriguez, Director—Instructional Monitoring
FROM: Lemmie Wade, Principal
RE: POTENTIAL UNSATISFACTORY EVALUATION

During November 20XX, observations were conducted in all teachers' classrooms.
I observed Mr. Anthony on

Day	Date	Time
Monday	November 1, 20XX	9:15-10:00 A.M.
Thursday	November 11, 20XX	10:30-11:30 A.M.
Wednesday	November 17, 20XX	1:30-2:30 P.M.
Monday	November 22, 20XX	8:00-9:00 A.M.
Tuesday	November 23, 20XX	9:00-10:00 A.M.

These observations represent a reasonable sampling and included all aspects of
Mr. Anthony's assignment, morning and afternoon.

During the postobservation conferences, Mr. Anthony's strengths and weaknesses were discussed. In addition, I offered suggestions for improvement,
described the assistance available, and set a reasonable period of time for necessary improvement.

Enclosed is a copy of the summary letter dated November 23, 20XX, and given
to Mr. Anthony offering specific suggestions for improvement. Also enclosed are
copies of the formal and informal evaluation forms used to observe Mr. Anthony.

I have continued to use the same formal and informal evaluation forms that were
presented to all teachers on September 1, 20XX, in a letter explaining the evaluation process at Kennedy Elementary School.

cc: Calvin P. Thompson, Attorney at Law—ABC School District

Enclosures

ABC SCHOOL DISTRICT   **KENNEDY ELEMENTARY SCHOOL**

1584 South Pineview Drive
Crescent Ridge, California 70799
(916) 444-4444

DATE: December 14, 20XX
TO: Dr. Derek Rodriguez, Director-Instructional Monitoring
FROM: Lemmie Wade, Principal
RE: POTENTIAL UNSATISFACTORY EVALUATION

During December 20XX, formal and informal observations conducted in all teachers' classrooms. I observed Mr. Anthony on

Day	Date	Time
Wednesday	December 1, 20XX	8:00-8:45 A.M.
Tuesday	December 7, 20XX	10:45-11:30 A.M.
Friday	December 10, 20XX	9:20-10:15 A.M.
Monday	December 13, 20XX	1:00-1:30 P.M.

These observations represent a reasonable sampling and included Mr. Anthony's assignment, morning and afternoon.

During the postobservation conferences, Mr. Anthony's strengths and weaknesses were discussed. In addition I offered suggestions for improvement, described the assistance available, and set a reasonable period of time for necessary improvement.

Enclosed is a copy of the summary letter dated December 14, 20XX, and given to Mr. Anthony offering specific suggestions for improvement. Also enclosed are copies of the formal and informal evaluation forms used to observe Mr. Anthony.

I have used the same formal and informal evaluation forms that were presented to all teachers on September 1, 20XX, with a letter explaining the evaluation process at Kennedy Elementary School. I am planning to issue an unsatisfactory teacher evaluation if Mr. Anthony does not improve and would like for you to review my documentation before it is finalized.

cc: Calvin P. Thompson, Attorney at Law—ABC School District

Enclosures

ABC SCHOOL DISTRICT   **KENNEDY ELEMENTARY SCHOOL**

1584 South Pineview Drive
Crescent Ridge, California 70799
(916) 444-4444

December 17, 20XX

Mr. William Anthony
Kennedy Elementary School

Dear Mr. Anthony:

From the beginning of September through December of the 20XX-20XX school year, formal and informal observations were made of your classroom. Specifically, I observed you on

Day	Date	Time
Wednesday	September 8, 20XX	8:00-8:25 A.M.
Friday	September 10, 20XX	10:20-10:30 A.M.
Tuesday	September 14, 20XX	1:10-1:25 P.M.
Monday	September 20, 20XX	2:15-2:30 P.M.
Wednesday	September 22, 20XX	2:45-3:00 P.M.
Monday	September 27, 20XX	8:10-8:30 A.M.
Friday	October 1, 20XX	9:15-10:10 A.M.
Wednesday	October 6, 20XX	8:05-9:00 A.M.
Tuesday	October 12, 20XX	10:15-11:05 A.M.
Tuesday	October 19, 20XX	9:10-10:20 A.M.
Monday	November 1, 20XX	9:15-10:00 A.M.
Thursday	November 11, 20XX	10:30-11:30 A.M.
Wednesday	November 17, 20XX	1:30-2:30 P.M.
Monday	November 22, 20XX	8:00-9:00 A.M.
Tuesday	November 23, 20XX	9:00-10:00 A.M.
Wednesday	December 1, 20XX	8:00-8:45 A.M.
Tuesday	December 7, 20XX	10:45-11:30 A.M.
Friday	December 10, 20XX	9:20-10:15 A.M.
Monday	December 13, 20XX	1:00-1:30 P.M.

These observations represent a reasonable sampling of your teaching performance and included all aspects of your assignment, morning and afternoon.

In addition to memoranda that were sent to you outlining my concerns, I held conferences with you to discuss deficiencies, available assistance, and suggestions for improvement, as well as setting a reasonable time for necessary improvement. Letters summarizing our conferences were sent to you on October 27, November 23, and December 14, 20XX.

X-B

Unfortunately, at this time, your teaching performance has not improved to a satisfactory level. Therefore this letter serves as official notification that failure to achieve a satisfactory level of performance by January 14, 20XX, will result in the issuance of an unsatisfactory evaluation with a recommendation for your dismissal from the ABC School District.

Sincerely,

Lemmie Wade, PhD
Principal

ABC SCHOOL DISTRICT   **KENNEDY ELEMENTARY SCHOOL**

1584 South Pineview Drive
Crescent Ridge, California 70799
(916) 444-4444

January 14, 20XX

Mr. William Anthony
Kennedy Elementary School

Dear Mr. Anthony:

This letter is to inform you that I plan to submit an unsatisfactory teacher evaluation for you to the Department of School Personnel. I will give you a copy of this evaluation on Thursday, January 20, 20XX, at 3:15 P.M. in my office.

The Master Contract, Part III, Section A, on pages 15 and 16, governs the due process of teacher performance evaluations. If you wish, you may be represented by a member of your bargaining unit or other person of your choice.

After the conference, you will be allowed 72 hours to study my comments and respond to them in writing. The unsatisfactory evaluation will then be filed with the Department of School Personnel with a recommendation for your dismissal from the ABC School District.

Sincerely,

Lemmie Wade, PhD
Principal

ABC SCHOOL DISTRICT

KENNEDY ELEMENTARY SCHOOL

1584 South Pineview Drive
Crescent Ridge, California 70799
(916) 444-4444

January 18, 20XX

Mr. William Anthony
Kennedy Elementary School

Dear Mr. Anthony:

This memorandum is to remind you about our meeting, which is scheduled for Thursday, January 20, 20XX, at 3:15 P.M. in my office. The purpose of this meeting is to discuss the issuance of an unsatisfactory teacher evaluation to you.

If you wish, you may be represented by a bargaining unit representative or anyone of your choice.

Sincerely,

Lemmie Wade, PhD
Principal

ABC SCHOOL DISTRICT   **KENNEDY ELEMENTARY SCHOOL**

1584 South Pineview Drive
Crescent Ridge, California 70799
(916) 444-4444

TEACHER PERFORMANCE EVALUATION

DATE January 20, 20XX

NAME   William Anthony   SUBJECT/GRADES   5th

SCHOOL   Kennedy Elementary School   YEAR   20XX-20XX

Principals and other personnel delegated by position or assignment to evaluate the performance of the teacher are requested to complete the evaluation form. In the space provided, include a statement that supports the assessment.

In my professional judgment, Mr. William Anthony is not making a satisfactory contribution to the educational program at Kennedy Elementary School. It is recommended that he be dismissed from the school district next semester because

1. He has failed to provide a safe learning environment for his students.
2. He has failed to develop an effective behavioral management plan to reduce negative student behavior.
3. He has failed to develop and implement effective lesson plans.
4. He has failed to provide meaningful instruction for his students.
5. He has failed to respond to efforts that were made to help improve his teaching performance.

Lemmie Wade, PhD   Principal
_____   _____
Evaluator   Title

(NOTE: The district evaluation form should be used.)

X-E

ABC SCHOOL DISTRICT   **KENNEDY ELEMENTARY SCHOOL**

1584 South Pineview Drive
Crescent Ridge, California 70799
(916) 444-4444

CLOSING STATEMENT

Unfortunately, Mr. William Anthony's overall teaching performance is related to undesirable student behaviors. Mr. Anthony failed to respond to the efforts that were made to help improve his teaching performance and he failed to develop a classroom management plan to reduce negative student behavior. These are justifications for issuing an unsatisfactory teacher evaluation.

Therefore I am recommending that Mr. William Anthony be relieved of his teaching responsibilities at Kennedy Elementary School and that he be terminated from the ABC School District, effective at the end of the 20XX-20XX school year.

(NOTE: This statement should not be included in the Unsatisfactory Teacher Document. It should be read at the end of each hearing.)

RESOURCE

Supplemental Forms and Letters

In addition to the documents provided in the sample Unsatisfactory Teacher Evaluation Documentation, the following forms and letters were used in the total evaluation process.

SUPPLEMENTAL FORMS AND LETTERS USED IN CONJUNCTION WITH THE
UNSATISFACTORY TEACHER EVALUATION OF

WILLIAM ANTHONY

KENNEDY ELEMENTARY SCHOOL

CHECKLIST FOR COLLECTING HISTORICAL INFORMATION
KENNEDY ELEMENTARY SCHOOL
20XX-20XX

Teacher: William Anthony

❏ Contact the personnel department to verify the teacher's area of certification.

❏ Check the teacher's personnel file and read previous letters warning the teacher about unsatisfactory teaching performance. Note the dates and the name(s) of the principal(s).

❏ Check the teacher's personnel file and read previous teacher evaluation documents. Carefully read for written comments about unsatisfactory teaching performance or warnings given by previous principals as well as comments providing suggestions for improvement. Note the dates and the name(s) of the principal(s).

❏ Check the local school file for any written warnings about an unsatisfactory teacher evaluation. Note the dates and the name(s) of the principal(s).

❏ Check local school records to find out the number of days the teacher has been absent and the number of times the teacher has been late to work as related to an unsatisfactory teacher evaluation.

❏ Contact the personnel department to find out the number of days the teacher has been absent during the past three years.

❏ Check the local school file for any misconduct charges against the teacher as related to an unsatisfactory teacher evaluation.

❏ Contact the department responsible for workers' compensation to determine if the teacher has filed claims for workers' compensation as related to an unsatisfactory teacher evaluation.

KENNEDY ELEMENTARY SCHOOL
SUMMARY OF STRENGTHS AND AREAS OF NEED OF TEACHING STAFF:
20XX-20XX

Staff Member	Classroom Management	Classroom Instruction	Lesson Planning	High Student Expectations
Adams, Hilda				
Anthony, William				
Barnett, Michelle				
Craine, Diane				
Dailey, Dawna				
Elliott, Lucia				
Haggerty, Faye				
Hall, Rachel				
Hernandez, Rosa				
Huebner, Shelly				
Larson, Scott				
Maas-Carns, Camille				
Margis, Cindy				
McNeal, Donald				
Najam, Sara				
O'Donnell, Marlene				
Patterson, Gary				
Thomas, Stewart				
Williams, Darren				
Zwicke, Gail				

References

Lawrence, C., & Vachon, M. (1995). *How to handle staff misconduct: A step-by-step guide.* Thousand Oaks, CA: Corwin.

Lawrence, C., & Vachon, M. (1997). *The incompetent specialist: How to evaluate, document performance, and dismiss school staff.* Thousand Oaks, CA: Corwin.

CORWIN PRESS

The Corwin Press logo—a raven striding across an open book—represents the happy union of courage and learning. We are a professional-level publisher of books and journals for K–12 educators, and we are committed to creating and providing resources that embody these qualities. Corwin's motto is "Success for All Learners."